CHARLES MESSENGER

ARMIES OF
WORLD WAR 3

CHARLES MESSENGER
ARMIES OF WORLD WAR 3

THE MILITARY PRESS
Distributed by Crown Publishers Inc.
New York
A Bison Book

This edition is published by
The Military Press, distributed by
Crown Publishers Inc.

Produced by
Bison Books Corp.
17 Sherwood Place
Greenwich, CT 06830
USA

Printed in Hong Kong

ISBN 0-517-42501-7

h g f e d c b a

CONTENTS

US border patrol on the Inner German Border near Fulda.

1. NATO AND THE WARSAW PACT

May 1945 saw the Soviet Union and the Western Allies standing triumphant on the soil of defeated Nazi Germany. At Potsdam in July of that year, Premier Stalin, President Truman and Prime Minister Attlee agreed on the dismemberment of Germany into Allied zones of occupation, while at the same time the United Nations was set up at the San Francisco Conference in an attempt to prevent future armed conflict. There was, however, growing concern among the Western Allies over the Soviet treatment of the territories of Eastern Europe. Civil War in Greece and China also pointed to the expansionist threat of communism. Then, in March 1946, Winston Churchill made his famous speech at Fulton, Missouri, in which he spoke of 'an iron curtain [that] has descended across the continent' and called for concerted Anglo-American action to prevent the tide of communism flowing further westward.

Attempts throughout 1946 to bring about a formal peace which would end World War II resulted in drawn out haggling between the Soviet Union and her wartime allies. When agreement was finally reached at the Paris Conference and treaties signed in February 1947, Russian domination over Eastern Europe was seemingly confirmed. The fact, too, that from a very early stage the Russians in their zone of occupation refused to cooperate with the West also

Above: Marshal Tito of Yugoslavia.
Below: The Reichstag, Berlin on 7 May 1945, the day of Germany's final surrender.
Right: Eisenhower and Churchill, Christmas Day 1943.

added to the growing feeling that Churchill's iron curtain was indeed real. There was also early realization by the Truman administration that weak economies could hasten the onset of communism. Thus in mid-1946, Congress approved a loan to Britain in order to help her convert her economy from war to peace, and further loans were discussed for Greece, and Turkey, who was being threatened by Soviet takeover of two eastern provinces. This culminated in the Truman Doctrine, when in March 1947 the President announced that the United States was prepared to use its resources to help any country threatened by communism, and economic and military aid to Greece and Turkey was approved.

It was clear now that the USA could not return to her prewar isolationism, and that the spread of revolution throughout the world was against her interests. As a first step, war-ravaged Western Europe needed to be built up, and in June 1947 Secretary of State George C Marshall proposed that the USA give material aid to the European nations in order to help them set up on a firm peacetime footing. No specific invitation was issued to Stalin, but the offer was clear in that it extended to all European nations which had suffered in the war. Stalin, however, saw this as a capitalist plot to enslave the whole of Europe and ignored it. The western European nations seized upon it eagerly, including neutral Sweden and Switzerland, and in April 1948 the European Recovery Program, or Marshall Plan, as it is more commonly called, was put into effect. In the meantime, Stalin tightened his control over the satellite governments of Eastern Europe.

Yugoslavia under Tito stood out against him, but elsewhere there were purges and, in Czechoslovakia, a naked coup d'état in February 1948 which placed in power a government suitably subservient to Moscow.

The London Protocol signed by the USSR, USA and Britain in September 1944 had drawn up the original zones of occupation, and had agreed that Berlin should be divided separately. At Yalta, in February 1945, the French were also invited to participate, and this resulted in both Germany and Berlin being divided into four zones, but that the latter would be under the combined government of the Allied Kommandantura. It was clear, though, from very early on that the Russians would only cooperate over Berlin when it suited them to do so.

Matters got steadily worse, and in Spring 1948 the Russians tried to impose the East Berlin mark as the only allowable currency for the city. The Western powers objected, and on 25 June 1948 they sealed off all the land access routes to West Berlin. This marked the start of the Berlin blockade. It was to continue until May the following year, and the inhabitants of West Berlin were only prevented from starving through a massive airlift of supplies.

The Czech coup d'état and the Berlin blockade were stark indications of the threat of Soviet communism, and it was this that brought about the setting up of the North Atlantic Treaty Organization (NATO) in April 1949. The founding nations were twelve in all – United States, Canada, Great Britain, France, the Netherlands, Belgium, Luxembourg, Italy, Norway, Denmark, Iceland and Portugal. They agreed to come to one another's aid in the event of attack, to consult periodically on military and economic subjects, and to set up a unified military command system, to which each member nation would contribute forces. Later, other countries would join – Greece and Turkey in 1951, the Federal Republic of Germany in 1955, and Spain in 1982.

The formation of NATO seemed initially to result in a reduction of tension in Europe. The USSR raised the Berlin blockade, and in that same month, May 1949, the French, British, Soviet and US Foreign Ministers met in Paris and managed to resolve a number of problems over Germany and

Berlin, as well as on the question of a peace treaty with Austria. Finally, in October 1949, the Albanians and Bulgarians gave up giving active support to the Greek communists, and the three year civil war in Greece came to an end. In the meantime, the NATO members began detailed planning for a strategy for the defense of Europe.

Then, in June 1950 the North Koreans invaded South Korea, and US and other UN forces went to the aid of the latter. North Korea had, after the war become very much part of the Soviet sphere of influence, and her attack on her neighbor was seen as an indication that Soviet expansion was on the move once more. This combined with the successful exploding of a Soviet A-bomb in 1949, lent added urgency to NATO military planning, and in December 1950 General Dwight D Eisenhower was formally appointed as the first Supreme Allied Commander Europe (SACEUR), and he established his headquarters (Supreme Headquarters Allied Powers Europe (SHAPE)) at Rocquencourt near Paris at the beginning of the following April. Not until February 1952, however, did the Alliance agree at Lisbon that the forces it required were fifty divisions, 4000 aircraft and strong naval forces. On the political front, it had been realized from the outset that the Alliance would be considerably strengthened if West Germany, where the main battle was likely to be fought, was allowed to participate in the defence of Western Europe. By the end of 1949 the basis of a West

Left: Korea – US Marines in the Chosin Reservoir area, December 1950.
Above: Korea – Captured Chinese, November 1950. Red China's involvement made Washington believe that World War 3 was about to begin.

German state had been agreed, and Konrad Adenauer became the first Chancellor of the new Federal Republic of Germany (FRG). Simultaneously, the Russians set up the German Democratic Republic (GDR). During 1950 and 1951 exploratory talks were held between the Allied Commissioners and the FRG Government, but they came to nothing, mainly because of internal differences in the FRG and the fact that the French, rather than see an FRG army *per se*, preferred the idea of a European Army, the Pleven Plan, with West German units integrated at battalion level. Nevertheless, the European Coal and Steel Community, the forerunner to the European Economic Community was set up in April 1951, with Belgium, France, Italy, Luxembourg, the Netherlands and FRG as members.

1953 was marked by a number of events, some of which reduced tension, while others raised it. First and foremost was the death on 5 March of Stalin. The subsequent partial dismantlement of the Soviet terror system, which included amnesties for some categories of political prisoner, the Korean Armistice and Soviet establishment of diplomatic relations with Israel, Yugoslavia and Greece, all seemed to indicate that Soviet policy was becoming less aggressive. Yet,

on the other hand, the severity with which food riots in Berlin were put down that summer and the Soviet announcement that she now had the H-bomb, put the West in two minds. Furthermore, although the West believed that Germany should, at some stage in the future, be reunified, the Soviet Union would only agree to this in the early Fifties, if all occupying forces were withdrawn within one year of this, and that the government should be a coalition of the two existing governments. This was unacceptable in the West, as they foresaw a communist takeover of the country. Then at a conference between the four major Powers held in Berlin in early 1954, the Western Powers proposed free elections in both Germanies in order to set up a unified government, but this was rejected out of hand by the Soviet Union.

Up until 1954, NATO had based its plans on the defense of the Central Region on building up sufficient conventional forces, but it was quite clear that the Lisbon aims would not be met because of the strain on national economies. During 1953, therefore, Admiral Radford, Chairman of the US Joint Chiefs of Staff evolved the concept that the USA and its allies should base their defense on the commitment to use nuclear weapons. This was accepted by President Eisenhower at the end of October 1953, first broadcast by John Foster Dulles in January 1954, and agreed as alliance policy at the end of that year. Any war with the Soviet Union within the NATO area could no longer be limited, and such conventional forces as there were would merely act as a trip wire, which once crossed by the Soviets would result in the release of tactical and strategic nuclear weapons. This was the policy of Massive Retaliation, designed, as President Eisenhower said, to achieve 'more bang for the buck' and counteract Soviet conventional force superiority in Europe.

The Soviet Union, however, was more concerned about other events. Indeed, Dulles had recognized as early as April 1954 that the United States must not get herself in a position where the only course open was general war, and Eisenhower's resolve at the same time not to allow the communists to overrun Indo-China soon evaporated when the French were defeated there, and the USA acquiesced to the agreement at the Geneva Conference that she should withdraw from the region. Instead the USA set up a number of blocs similar to NATO in order to contain any further Soviet expansion, and this resulted in the Manila and Baghdad Pacts and the extending of a nuclear guarantee to Nationalist China. To the Russians these moves seemed anything but defensive. Yet worse was to come, when the FRG was formally admitted to NATO at the beginning of May 1955, with the agreement that she should raise twelve divisions as her contribution to the Alliance. Two days later the USSR tore up her treaties with France and Britain, and on 14 May 1955 announced the formation of the Warsaw Pact with her European satellites as a direct counter to the FRG inclusion in NATO. Though it was not until the end of the year that she signed a treay with the Pankow regime in the GDR formally granting it the prerogatives of a state, and only at the end of January 1956 was the GDR admitted to the Warsaw Pact.

At the same time, there was a thawing of relations. Nikita Krushchev, First Secretary of the Soviet Communist Party, and, by 1955, the most powerful man in Russia, made a number of trips abroad that year, and in May 1955 the Austrian State Treaty ended the occupation of that country by the Four Powers. The price of this was Austrian neutralism, though, and it had the effect of geographically splitting NATO.

There was also a Soviet exchange with the US on agricultural expert visits, and Russian delegates attended a US inspired conference on the peaceful uses of nuclear energy. Then, in February 1956, at the Twentieth Congress of the Communist Party of the Soviet Union, Krushchev denounced the Stalin 'cult of personality'. But 1956 saw unrest among the satellites. Riots in Poland in July led to the appointment of Wladislaw Gomulka, who had been imprisoned in Stalin's time, as premier, and the sacking of the Soviet Marshal Rokossovsky as Minister of Defense. For a time it looked as though the Soviets might invade Poland, but talks between Kruschev and Gomulka resulted in a compromise, with the Russians having to accept a small measure of Polish independence. Then, unrest sprang up in Hungary, but this was more serious and led to fighting between Hungarians and Soviet troops stationed in the country. At the end of October, the Russians appeared to back down and agree the formation of a government under Imre Nagy, which included two non-communists. Nagy was about to declare Hungary's neutrality and take her out of the Warsaw Pact, when, on 4 November 1956, Soviet forces invaded.

For NATO this could not have come at a worse moment. A week before, the Israelis had invaded Egyptian held Sinai, and on 31 October, Anglo-French forces had attacked Egypt as a long delayed

Above left: Prime Minister Eden and President Nasser of Egypt in 1955. Anglo-French involvement at Suez in 1956 enabled the Soviets to intervene in Hungary and caused severe US disapproval.
Left: British Centurion tank lands at Suez, November 1956.
Above: East-West thaw? – Premier Krushchev arrives in USA, September 1959.

reaction to the nationalization of the Suez Canal by President Nasser. American disapproval of this action was strong, and with the alliance in such disarray no positive action to counter the Soviet crushing of the Hungarian uprising was possible. All NATO could do was to make sympathetic noises and care for the flood of refugees. It demonstrated that the Soviet Union was not prepared to countenance much independence of thought or action in Eastern Europe.

The late Fifties saw the dominant issue as Berlin, but this was merely a demonstration of Soviet resentment that, whereas the FRG had been officially recognized by most countries in the world, the GDR was only so acknowledged by those in the Communist Bloc. The Soviet ploy was to give the GDR control of the access routes from Berlin to the west, which would force formal Western acknowledgement that the GDR existed as a state. To this, the Western Powers would not agree. This culminated in the building of the Berlin Wall in August 1961, which was portrayed as a unified action by all the Warsaw Pact states to 'check the subversive actions against the countries of the Socialist camp'. Yet, the year before,

the USA had suffered embarrassment when the Soviets shot down a U-2 spy plane piloted by Capt Gary Powers on 1 May 1960, and the Americans were forced to agree to the cancelation of further such flights.

These continuing crises caused more and more people to question the doctrine of Massive Retaliation during the late Fifties and early Sixties. General Lauris Norstad, who had assumed as SACEUR in November 1956, was one of these. He was particularly concerned that the Warsaw Pact might mount a limited conventional attack on the flanks of NATO, against Scandinavia or Greece or Turkey. If this did happen, he queried whether it would be worth launching a massive nuclear retaliatory strike in retaliation and thus precipitating a global nuclear war. As a result, during 1959–60 the Allied Command Europe Mobile Force (ACE Mobile Force or AMF) was set up. This was a small conventionally equipped multinational force capable of quick deployment in time of tension. Because it was multinational, its deterrence power lay in the fact that it was a demonstration of NATO solidarity. As for Norstad's overall military policy, while attempts would be made initially to resist Warsaw Pact aggression with conventional forces, should this fail he saw tactical nuclear weapons being used in a very selective fashion. It was hoped that this would make the Warsaw Pact pause and reconsider.

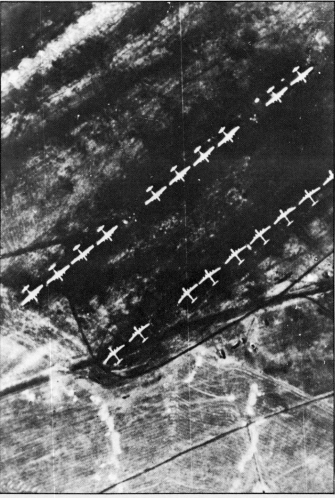

It was the Cuban missile crisis of Autumn 1962 which brought tension to a head. President Kennedy's ultimatum to Krushchev to remove his missiles from Cuba or take the consequences, brought the world the closest it had been to a global war since 1945. Krushchev backed down, and this marked the beginnings of a thaw. A year later, in August 1963, the USA and Soviet Union agreed to a Partial Nuclear Test Ban Treaty, and also to set up a Hot Line telephone system between Washington and Moscow.

In October 1963 the Americans launched Operation *Big Lift*, which was designed to demonstrate how quickly Europe could be reinforced from the Continental United States (CONUS), and 14,500 troops were airlifted across the Atlantic in record time. The Sixties, however, saw US eyes turning more and more towards South East Asia as she became ever more deeply embroiled in Vietnam. Within the context of overall NATO strategy, the decade did, however, bring about major changes. The growing concern over the viability of Massive Retaliation led to the development of a new doctrine, that of Flexible Response. The architect of this was Secretary of State Robert McNamara. He advocated the creation of a balanced force, with a mix of conventional and nuclear capabilities, which would be able to react to a range of crises without necessarily being committed to an immediate nuclear response, although this would remain the ultimate weapon. It did have its critics, especially in Europe, which, with NATO forces still markedly inferior in the conventional sense to those of the Warsaw Pact in terms of numbers of men and amount of materiel, was heavily reliant on the US strategic nuclear weapon. Their fear was that, since the Soviets did not consider that a limited tactical nuclear war was possible, nuclear weapons therefore counted for little, and Western Europe might be overrun before the US strategic weapon was brought into play. Nevertheless, the overwhelming argument that Flexible Response reduced the risk of a global nuclear holocaust eventually won the day, and the concept was adopted as official NATO policy in 1967.

A further major military decision made that year was the introduction of the Policy of Forward Defense. In the early days of NATO, it had been accepted that the overwhelming Soviet conventional superiority in Europe might well lead to the quick overrunning of the FRG, and it was envisaged that the main defense line might have to rest on the Rhine. After 1955, the FRG, now a member of NATO, expressed natural and increasing concern over the Alliance's seeming willingness to surrender her territory with little fight. As a result, the main defense line was moved forward to the line of the Rivers Weser and Lech. Only once this had been breached, would the use of tactical nuclear weapons be considered, and Warsaw Pact forces would be canalized

Above left: Gary Powers, whose shooting down set back Soviet/US relations.
Left: Soviet released photograph taken by Powers of Russian airfield. Left hand aircraft row is unidentifiable, while right hand appears to be prewar TB-3 bombers. It may have been a fake.
Above: Cuba 1962 – Soviet freighter with possible missiles on deck approaching the island.

into nuclear killing zones, where they would present a worthwhile tactical nuclear target. This still implied the surrender of significant portions of West German territory, and the FRG demanded agreement that determined defense of the whole of the country must be agreed, and this was accepted by the Alliance as a whole.

Within the Alliance, the Sixties also saw French withdrawal from active military participation in NATO. President de Gaulle, who had come to power in 1958 in order to deal with the Algerian crisis, had a vision of a Europe of nationally self-conscious states led by a France reawakened after the dents caused to her morale by Indo-China and Algeria. He saw the USA as being too dominant, and wanted France to pursue a more independent line. He refused, unlike the British, to commit the French independent nuclear deterrent to NATO and also did not sign the 1963 Partial Test Ban Treaty. Finally, in 1966 France's military contribution to NATO was withdrawn, although French troops remained in their

traditional zone of occupation in the FRG. Her political ties with the Alliance, however, remained unchanged. One of the immediate results of this was that all NATO military installations in France had to be moved, and a new location for SHAPE was found at Mons in Belgium.

The mid-Sixties saw further progress towards detente, and a major driving force behind this was the FRG Foreign Minister Willy Brandt. He believed that the dangers facing West Germany could be reduced if a better relationship with the East was built up, and this policy became known as *Ostpolitik*. He had early successes in establishing diplomatic relations with Romania, which was drawing away from active involvement in the Warsaw Pact and forging industrial links with the West. Nevertheless, there was concern among the other Warsaw Pact members, especially the GDR, who saw herself being isolated by *Ostpolitik*. Consequently, it was agreed that no Warsaw Pact member would establish diplomatic relations with the Federal Republic without prior agreement with the GDR. There were also moves to reduce the nuclear tension, and these culminated in the signing of the Non-Proliferation Treaty on Nuclear Weapons, and the opening of negotiations between the Soviets and the US on strategic arms limitations (SALT). Both these events occurred in 1970.

15

One event in the late Sixties did cause a momentary pause in the march towards detente. At the beginning of 1968 Antonin Novotny, a Stalinist of the old school, was forced to resign his position as First Secretary of the Czech Communist Party, and was replaced by a liberal, Alexander Dubček. This brought about the 'Prague Spring' with marked relaxations on the press and greater freedom of speech. The resultant criticisms of the previous regime were seen by the Soviet Union as being directed against herself, and she became increasingly concerned. As a warning, the Polish-Czech frontier was closed in May and joint Soviet-Polish maneuvers took place close to it. This was followed by Soviet Premier Kosygin and Marshal Grechko, Commander-in-Chief of the Warsaw Pact forces, visiting Prague. While the Czechs assured the Soviet Union of their continued friendship and that they still remained a loyal member of the Warsaw Pact, no steps were taken to halt the liberalization of the country. Meanwhile, the Pact maneuvers continued and a letter was sent to the Czechs warning them of the dangers of 'anti-socialist forces' taking control of the country. By now, however, the situation had become too serious for the Soviet Union to allow it to continue, especially since she was afraid that the unrest might spill over into Poland and the GDR. Thus, on 20 August Warsaw Pact forces made up of Soviet, Polish, East German, Bulgarian and Hungarian troops invaded Czechoslovakia, and deposed Dubček. There was, unlike in 1956, no violent resistance.

Apart from the display of Warsaw Pact solidarity towards the erring member state and the speed of the operation, it also caught NATO unprepared once more. The Alliance was well aware of the build up of the crisis over the summer months, but August is the traditional holiday month in the West, and the Pact did not move until it knew that President Johnson had departed from Washington on his vacation. Furthermore, the Soviets had rightly identified Prague as the key to the country and the first move had been the landing of troops at the airport in order to seize key government installations. Surprise was complete, and all NATO could do was to denounce the invasion as contrary to the principles of the United Nations Charter, and to resolve to improve the state of NATO forces. As for the Soviet justification for their actions, this became enshrined in the Brezhnev Doctrine, when the First Secretary stated, in November 1968, that a threat to socialism in one Warsaw Pact country was a threat to the Pact as a whole.

The Seventies began with much progress in detente. Besides SALT and the Non-Proliferation Treaty, 1970 also saw Four Power talks open on the future of Berlin, and these resulted in the signing of the first stage of a quadripartite agreement in September 1971, the first on Berlin since 1949. This re-affirmed the Four Power responsibility for the City,

Left: Prague, August 1968.
Below: A further round of SALT II talks. Soviet and US delegates, May 1977.

Above: Typical North German Plain terrain with British armor maneuvering.
Right: Both alliances must be prepared to fight in Arctic conditions.

and guaranteed uninterrupted civilian access between the Western sector and East Berlin. In May 1972, an interim agreement of strategic arms limitations (SALT I) was signed in Moscow, and SALT II talks got underway in Geneva towards the end of that year. The next year saw the beginning of the Mutual and Balanced Force Reductions (MBFR) talks, which were designed to reduce NATO and Warsaw Pact military forces in Europe. Running parallel to these were the Conference on Security and Cooperation in Europe (CSCE) talks at Helsinki, Finland, also designed to encourage detente. Further, in June 1973 Leonid Brezhnev and President Nixon met for talks in Washington and declared that they had both agreed on the prevention of nuclear war.

Yet, in spite of these encouraging signs that relations between East and West were improving, there were still causes for concern. Soviet military strength in Western eyes continued to grow, and NATO resolved to improve its conventional defenses accordingly. Then, at the end of 1973 came the sudden announcement by the Organization of Petroleum Exporting Countries (OPEC) that the six oil producing Persian Gulf states were doubling their prices of crude oil. In addition, there was continuing unrest in the Middle East, which culminated in the Yom

Kippur War of October 1973. That year also marked the beginning of a decade of world economic recession. The Turkish invasion of Cyprus in July 1974 caused Greece, like France before her, to withdraw from the integrated military NATO structure, although she rejoined six years later.

SALT II was finally signed in Vienna in June 1979 by President Carter and Leonid Brezhnev. In Christmas week of that same year, however, the Soviet Union intervened militarily in Afghanistan, and partially as a result the US Senate refused to ratify SALT II. Earlier, in 1977, NATO had noticed the build-up of Soviet intermediate range mobile nuclear systems, especially the deployment of SS-20, and in 1979 the Alliance decided its own theater nuclear force should be modernized, and Pershing 2s and the Cruise missile would be deployed to Europe. In conjunction with this, an offer was made to the Soviets in 1981 that if they dismantled their SS-20s, then this deployment would not take place – what became commonly known as the 'Twin Track Decision'. Afghanistan and unrest in Poland and the

Middle East, and Russian refusal to back down on the SS-20 deployment have led to heightened tension and what many regard as the Second Cold War. There is therefore renewed interest in the dangers of war breaking out between the Warsaw Pact and NATO, particularly in Europe.

The armies of World War III sit facing one another along a line which stretches from the North Cape to Mt Ararat in Eastern Turkey. Norway, the most northerly of the NATO members, shares a common border of some 150 miles with the Soviet Union in the Arctic wastes of Finmark. She must also be aware of possible Soviet violation of the neutrality of Finland and Sweden and must watch her long borders with those two countries. Of joint concern to both Norway and her fellow NATO member to the south, Denmark, is the Skagerrak. This, as the only access from the Baltic into the Atlantic, is a natural maritime choke point and, without control of it, the Soviet Baltic Fleet is landlocked. Hence Southern Norway and Denmark are obvious objectives for seizure by the Warsaw Pact.

Crossing the Danish border into Schleswig-Holstein, the most northerly region of the Federal Republic of Germany, the River Elbe is reached. This provides a natural internal NATO boundary.

The bulk of West Germany adjoins the GDR and Czechoslovakia, and the border with these two Warsaw Pact members runs for 500 miles. The North German Plain is relatively flat with a number of rivers and canals crossing it, but south of Hannover the terrain becomes much hillier and more wooded. There are, however, a number of more open stretches within it, notably the Fulda Gap northeast of Frankfurt am Main, the area around Wurzburg and that north of Munich. The southern shoulder of the FRG rests against the Austrian and Swiss Alps, and these two countries provide another natural NATO border.

South of the Alps lies Italy, and her main concern is with the northeast. She must guard against an attack through Austria, as well as one through Yugoslavia into the lowlands north of Trieste. Yugoslavia and inward looking Albania create another gap in NATO's land defenses, but then comes Greece. Here the main concern is the 300 mile border with Bulgaria, but there is the problem of defending Thrace with the Aegean Sea as little as 50 miles in places from the border. Attacks through Albania and Yugoslavia cannot, however, be discounted. Finally, there is Turkey, whose combined coastal and land-locked border with the Warsaw Pact is, with a length of almost 2000 miles, by far the longest of any NATO member. In the north-east the maritime choke points of the Bosporus and the Dardanelles are, like the Skagerrak, crucial objectives for the Warsaw Pact, if the Black Sea Fleet is to play its role in the Mediterranean. Going eastwards, the Turkish border runs along the southern shore of the Black Sea, which is very much a Soviet 'pond', and then turns south through the mountainous and desert areas adjoining the Soviet Socialist Republics of Georgia and Armenia.

The frontage between the NATO and Warsaw Pact armies is too long and, in NATO's case, too split up, for one command to control operations throughout its length in any detail. Both sides have therefore divided it into a number of theaters. NATO regards Scandinavia, Denmark and Holstein as the Northern Flank, the remainder of the FRG as the Central Region, and everything south of the Alps as the Southern Flank. The Warsaw Pact has divided the area along similar geographic lines, and terms these sectors as Theaters of Military Operations (TMOs or, in Russian, TVDs). North equates to the NATO Northern Flank, although it does not include Denmark and Schleswig Holstein. Central Europe is equivalent to the Central Region, and Southwest Europe covers the Southern Flank. A fourth TMO, South, covers Iran, the Gulf and Afghanistan, while a fifth, which does not fall into the context of this book, is Far East and takes care of the Sino-Soviet border.

The description of how each alliance intends to fight the land battle will be set against the Central Region, since this has long been the focus of each side's attention. The general principles also apply to the flanks.

It is debatable as to how aggressive the Warsaw Pact really is. Nevertheless, if it is strictly defensive, as some argue, its military organization, equipment, and concept of operations are geared to the offense. The Soviet Union argues in terms of the 'counter offensive' as being the decisive operation in the land battle, and part of her military doctrine is the pre-emptive strike to be used, like the Israelis did in 1956 and 1967, to anticipate and prevent an attack on her. The two crucial elements of any such attack are speed and surprise. While the latter is designed to catch NATO off balance, the speed and momentum with which the offensive is carried out will prevent NATO forces from recovering from the shock of the initial blow. In particular, the Soviets look to early paralysis of NATO command, control and communications (C^3) systems, logistics installations and tactical nuclear weapons. The last of these is the most important, as the Soviets realize only too well that if NATO's conventional defense crumbles, they retain only the tactical nuclear option. Indeed, the Soviets, although they believe in equipping themselves to win a war at any level, would much prefer a quick conventional victory.

There is nothing radically new in this concept. Indeed much of it echoes the writings of those two eminent British military thinkers of the 1920s, Major General J F C Fuller and Captain B H Liddell Hart, and mirrors the German *blitzkrieg* tactics of 1939–41. However, while the mechanized forces of the Wehrmacht represented merely a steel tip to an army, which mainly marched on its feet and was reliant on horsedrawn transport, the Warsaw Pact armies of the 1980s are wholly mechanized or motorized. Yet, there are some recent developments to the doctrine which have made the West consider it more carefully than hitherto.

The concept of the Operational Maneuver Group (OMG) first appeared in the open press in the West in 1982. During World War II, in order to deal with strong German defenses on the Eastern Front, the Soviets developed the Mobile Group, which was used to exploit the initial success of the main attack. As the German defenses became deeper, it was realized that the Mobile Group was not enough to make a positive penetration. Therefore, the main attack was split into two echelons, with the second initially supporting the first, and then taking over once it was exhausted. In the postwar years, recognizing that NATO's conventional defenses in the Central Region appeared to lack depth, the Mobile Group was dispensed with, but the echelon system remained as a means of maintaining the momentum of the attack. During the Seventies, however, the Soviets became increasingly concerned over the growing plethora of anti-armor weapons on the battlefield, especially after examining the Yom Kippur war. There was concern that the offensive might become bogged down, and hence the Mobile Group was resurrected, but under a new name, the OMG. Its aim is slightly different, though, to its predecessor. It will be launched, probably on the first day of the offensive and certainly by the third. Its main object is to dislocate NATO C^3 assets by penetrating to the rear of the defenses and forcing Alliance troops to look in two directions at once. It will also seize and hold key terrain to facilitate the advance of second echelon forces.

An OMG will invariably be used in conjunction with air assault forces, either airborne or heliborne. The normal tactic would be for the OMG to link up with the latter once they are on the ground. Indeed, the growth of airborne and heliborne forces in the Warsaw Pact is very marked.

A final point which must be emphasized is that the strategic offensive carried out by a TMO consists of

Right above: Soviet BTR-60Ps on the march. They remain in column until just about to close with the enemy, when they will form a line abreast.
Right: Amphibious PT-76s come ashore. An outflanking amphibious attack behind NATO Central Region northern flank is very possible.

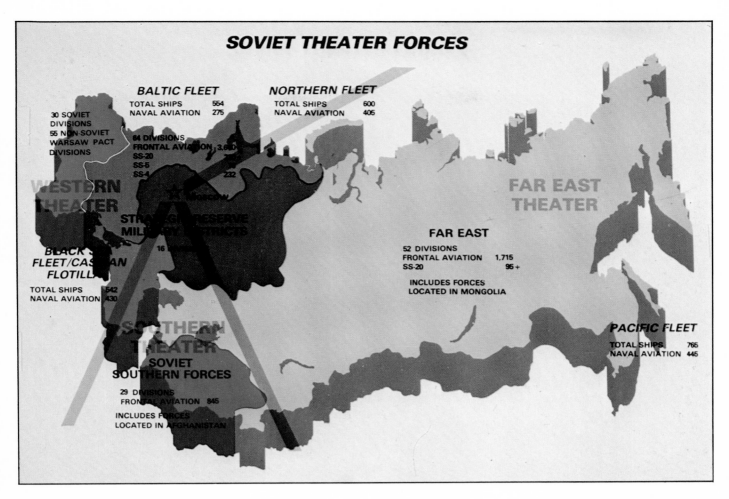

SOVIET THEATER FORCES

BALTIC FLEET
TOTAL SHIPS 554
NAVAL AVIATION 275

NORTHERN FLEET
TOTAL SHIPS 600
NAVAL AVIATION 405

30 SOVIET DIVISIONS
55 NON-SOVIET WARSAW PACT DIVISIONS

64 DIVISIONS
FRONTAL AVIATION 3,600
SS-20
SS-5
SS-4 232

WESTERN THEATER

STRATEGIC RESERVE MILITARY DISTRICTS 16

BLACK SEA FLEET/CASPIAN FLOTILLA
TOTAL SHIPS 542
NAVAL AVIATION 430

FAR EAST THEATER

FAR EAST
52 DIVISIONS
FRONTAL AVIATION 1,715
SS-20 96+

INCLUDES FORCES LOCATED IN MONGOLIA

PACIFIC FLEET
TOTAL SHIPS 765
NAVAL AVIATION 445

SOUTHERN THEATER

SOVIET SOUTHERN FORCES
29 DIVISIONS
FRONTAL AVIATION 845

INCLUDES FORCES LOCATED IN AFGHANISTAN

Left: East German Border Guards near Fulda, West Germany.
Above: Although the text speaks of a Northern and Central TMO, this US view reflects that both are combined into TMO West. This is an unresolved debate in Western defense circles.
Below: Soviet SD-44 antitank gun used by airborne units.

not just the ground offensive, but other operations as well. These will certainly include air, which is aimed at the destruction of NATO air and air defense assets, nuclear resources and associated C^3. Anti-air is designed to protect Warsaw Pact forces and to help achieve air superiority. Airborne and amphibious operations will be launched to secure areas of strategic importance, including maritime choke points, and to disrupt the enemy's government and higher military control. Finally, there are the naval operations aimed at destroying NATO naval forces at sea and in their bases, supporting operations ashore and securing maritime lines of communication.

The NATO concept of defense is designed to defeat any Warsaw Pact aggression in the Central Region as close as possible to the FRG's borders with the East. This is in line with the policy of Forward Defense. The Alliance hopes that it can achieve this with conventional means alone, but recognizes that it may be forced to use tactical nuclear weapons.

In essence, NATO forces conduct what is called Active Defense, which is a mixture of static and mobile. The conventional element consists of three parts. Covering forces will engage the enemy from the moment that they cross the border and fight a delaying action, as well as trying to identify the main axes of advance. In the meantime, the main defensive position will be prepared. It should be pointed out that

NATO does not employ pre-emplaced defenses, although in recent years a number of commentators have advocated this. The main problems are that any belt of fixed defenses might well be against the constitution of the FRG, which recognizes only one Germany and will countenance nothing which will impede the free movement of civilians in peacetime. In any event once these fortifications have been penetrated or enveloped, they are superfluous and hence there is a question mark on how cost effective they would be. Thus, NATO will prepare hasty defenses on deployment, and the covering force will attempt to buy time in order to perfect them.

The main defense line itself will be based on a natural obstacle as close as is tactically feasible to the border. It will be based very much on antiarmor weapons, and is designed to blunt the enemy attack by forcing him to pause, thereby losing momentum. It is, however, accepted that the enemy will eventually penetrate, and it is here that the third phase comes into play, counterpenetration and counterattack by reserve forces. Counterpenetration is the placing of forces in the path of a penetration, and will be particularly in evidence when dealing with OMGs. Counterattack, on the other hand, is physically attacking the enemy, ideally hitting him in the flank.

During these three phases reserve forces will be deployed from member countries, and the more time that these troops in place can hold, the more reserves will be deployed and the longer the conventional

NATO solidarity – US and Bundeswehr troops confer during Exercise Reforger. Will NATO national governments pull together in the same way in the event of a serious East-West crisis?

phase will last. If they cannot hold, then the decision must be made to use tactical nuclear weapons. This, however, will be an awesome one to make. Although, in theory it is hoped that making the nuclear strikes highly selective will force the Soviets to pause and reconsider, it is quite possible that the Soviets will retaliate in kind, and there is no guarantee that the nuclear exchange will not escalate. With these concerns in mind, the decision to grant tactical nuclear release will be a hard one for member countries to make, and by the time that they have made it, it might

well be too late.

It is these worries together with the fact that the NATO conventional defenses lack sufficient depth, which has led to some urgent rethinking and questioning as to the soundness of current NATO military doctrine. Distinguished military figures on both sides of the Atlantic have recently criticized the reliance on tactical nuclear weapons as a force multiplier, seeing this as lowering the nuclear threshold and making a global nuclear war more likely. Yet, if NATO is to have a more credible conventional defense, it must have more depth. The US has now come out with an answer to this, Airland Battle 2000. The key to this is extending depth forward rather than to the rear, and to concentrate on destroying the Warsaw Pact second echelon or follow-up forces. This is to be done in two ways. Air and ground forces, making maximum use of conventional Precision Guided Munitions (PGMs) will attack by fire, while mobile heliborne and mechanized forces will physically close with second echelon forces, crossing borders to do so. The basic philosophy behind this concept has already been enshrined in official US military thought, and, as we shall see, US Army equipment and structure is already being shaped accordingly. Airland Battle 2000 is heavily reliant on the exploitation of emerging technology (ET), especially in the fields of C^3 and intelligence (C^3I) and weapons, and many commentators believe that ET provides the key to NATO defense in the future. They argue that the Alliance is ahead of the Warsaw Pact in high technology and that it should take advantage of this, and use it as a force multiplier instead of the tactical nuclear weapon. However, Airland 2000 has not been officially accepted as NATO doctrine, and there is concern over it among European members.

The two major European worries are political and economic. The concept of physical strikes across the border is viewed as being in contradiction to NATO's strictly defensive posture, and such aggression might make a Soviet preemptive strike more rather than less likely, in that she will perceive Airland Battle 2000 as a threat. Secondly, high technology weapons systems are growing ever more expensive and are putting increasing strain on defense budgets. Indeed, the European members are finding it hard enough to achieve NATO goals laid down in 1979 for a 3% increase in defense expenditure in order to strengthen NATO's conventional capability. The US concept is therefore seen as putting even further pressure on budgets which are most unlikely to increase in size in the foreseeable future.

Thus, NATO's doctrine of defense is currently in a state of flux. The threat is realized only too clearly, and it is a question of finding a concept to counter it which is not merely militarily effective, but politically and economically acceptable as well.

Canadian infantry launch an attack from their Grizzly armored personnel carrier.

2. THE ARMIES LINE UP

In order to make a comprehensive evaluation of the armies of World War III, it is necessary to have an understanding of the higher command organizations of the two alliances. Clausewitz's often quoted dictum that war is a continuation of national policy is reflected in the structures of both, in that the highest policy making bodies of each are political rather than military.

NATO is headed by the North Atlantic Council which is made up of representatives of all member nations. These can either be permanent representatives or national ministers, dependent on what there is to be discussed. The Chairman is the Secretary General, appointed on the approval of all member states, and is currently Lord Carrington, Britain's former Foreign Secretary. All decisions are taken by common consent rather than majority vote. Below this comes the Defense Planning Committee (DPC), which is also chaired by the Secretary General and consists of a permanent representative from each of the member states in the integrated military structure, which excludes France. Below these two bodies come the civil and military structures. The former consists of a number of committees ranging from political and

economic affairs, science, armaments, nuclear planning and communications. The latter is the Military Committee, headed by a President, at the time of writing General Sverre Hamre of Norway, and a Chairman, Admiral Robert H Falls of Canada, as well as a Deputy Chairman. Each nation has a permanent military member who sits on the Committee, except for the French, who have a military mission and exercise a watching brief. The role of the Committee is to make recommendations to the Council and DPC on military matters, and to give guidance on military questions to Allied commanders and subordinate military authorities.

Below the Military Committee come the three major NATO Commands – Allied Command Europe (ACE), Allied Command Atlantic (ACLANT) and Allied Command Channel (ACCHAN). The last two named Commands are essentially maritime and outside the scope of this book. Allied Command Europe is commanded by SACEUR through SHAPE at Mons in Belgium. He is always an American, and is currently General Bernard W Rogers. He has five subordinate commands under him. To cover the Northern Flank is Allied Forces Northern Europe

Left: Soviet ASU-85 85mm tank destroyers.
Above: Soviet Naval Infantry dismount from a BTR-60P APC.

(AFNORTH) with Allied Forces North Norway, Allied Forces South Norway and Allied Forces Baltic Approaches under it. Headquarters is at Kolsos in Norway. Allied Forces Southern Europe (AFSOUTH) with headquarters at Naples, Italy, has five subordinate commands – Allied Land Forces Southern Europe, Allied Land Forces Southeastern Europe, Allied Air Forces Southern Europe, Allied Naval Forces Southern Europe and Naval Striking and Support Forces Southern Europe. The ACE Mobile Force is also directly under command of SACEUR and has its headquarters at Seckenheim in the FRG. Furthermore, the United Kingdom Air Forces Command (HQ High Wycombe, England) is also under SACEUR's direct control.

This leaves the Central Region, the focus of attention for this book. The Command responsible for this is Allied Forces Central Europe (AFCENT), which is based at Brunssum in the Netherlands. Under it come two army groups and two tactical air forces. The northern part of the region, with attention fixed mainly on the North German Plain, is covered by the Northern Army Group (NORTHAG) and supported by 2nd Allied Tactical Air Force (2 ATAF). Both headquarters are located at Rheindahlen near Moenchen Gladbach in Germany. NORTHAG has four national army corps under command, reading north to south, I Netherlands (NE) Corps, I German (GE) Corps, I British (BR) Corps and I Belgian (BE) Corps. In the south is Central Army Group (CENTAG), supported by 4 ATAF, with headquarters of both at Heidelburg. The four corps under command of CENTAG read from north to south as follows: III(GE) Corps, V(US) Corps, VII(US) Corps and II(GE) Corps.

The main difference between the Warsaw Pact and NATO higher command structures is that, whereas NATO defense policy is formulated as a result of consensus among the member states, that of the Pact is dictated by the Soviet Union, with the other member states having little influence. On the surface, nevertheless, this essential difference appears blurred. As NATO has its Council, so the Warsaw Pact is headed by the Political Consultative Committee, which has political representatives of the Pact member countries on it. Although, it is supposed to direct all Pact cultural, political and economic activities, it seldom meets more than once or twice a year, and has never been involved in major decision making. Below it appear the Combined Secretariat and the Permanent Commission. The former is responsible for logistics and armaments, including research and development (R&D) within the Pact,

Left: Soviet T-55s on the march.
Above: Soviet BMP mechanized infantry combat vehicles.

while the latter makes foreign policy recommendations to both the Political Consultative Committee and the Permanent Commission. There is also a Committee of Defense Ministers made up of the Defense Ministers of all Pact nations and always chaired by the Soviet Defense Minister. It is significant that all these bodies are based in Moscow. As for the military side of the higher organization, the Combined Supreme Command is headed by the Supreme Commander of the Combined Forces of the Warsaw Pact, who is always a Russian, and is currently Marshal of the Soviet Union Viktor G Kulikov. The Combined Supreme Command was based in Moscow until late 1971 when, as a sop to the other Pact members it was moved to Lvov in Poland. In peacetime it exercises command over all Russian ground and air forces based in the three most western Soviet Military Districts, all Soviet ground and air forces based in the satellite countries and all GDR air

and ground forces. In wartime, other Pact member forces would also come under its command. Its staff, including the Chief of Staff, is overwhelmingly Russian, although officers from other Pact countries do serve on it. The Supreme Commander also chairs the Military Council of the Warsaw Pact Forces, which is there to advise him on planning and operational aspects, and is made up of representatives of the member states.

Thus it will be seen that the Soviet Union exerts an iron grip on the Pact as a whole. Furthermore, the Supreme Commander is also a member of the Soviet Main Military Council, along with the Soviet Chief of Staff, 1st Deputy Defense Minister, 1st Deputy Chairman of the KGB and the Minister for Internal Affairs, and hence the Soviets can also influence the Pact through this route as well as through the Soviet Minister of Defense.

Under the Combined Supreme Command of the Warsaw Pact come the TMOs, and below them fronts. Each TMO has its own air force, made up of ground support, interdiction and helicopter elements, as well as an air defense force (PVO). Fronts equate to the NATO army groups. Thus the Central European Theater of Military Operations is likely to have three fronts, North, Central and Southwestern, which would be activated in wartime. As it is, the peacetime organization is very much built round the Groups of Soviet Forces based in the satellite countries. The most important of these is the Group of Soviet Forces Germany (GSFG), which is made up of five armies, comprising in total ten tank, ten motor rifle and one artillery division, as well as an air assault brigade. The headquarters of GSFG is at Zossen-Wunsdorf outside Berlin, and this would become the TMO HQ in wartime. Also under command of GSFG are two tank and four motor rifle divisions of the People's Army of the GDR. The Soviet Central Group of Forces based in Czechoslovakia (CGF) has two armies (three tank, three motor rifle divisions). The Soviet forces stationed in Hungary are known as the Southern Group of Forces (SGF), and its headquarters in Budapest would probably become the HQ of the Southwestern TMO. In Poland the Soviets have two motor rifle divisions based in the west of the country which make up the Northern Group of Forces (NGF). The NGF would be incorporated in the Central European TMO. As for the Northern TMO, two Soviet divisions are permanently based near the border with Norway, and the remainder would come, in time of war from the Leningrad Military District and the Baltic states.

All the Warsaw Pact armies are conscript, with the period of service being two years or eighteen months. For the Soviet Army the period is two years and conscripts are called up twice a year in May/June and November/December. Service is broken down into four six month periods. The first six months will see the conscript doing his basic military training and learning his trade, be it tank driver or radar operator. During this time conditions are harsh. If he is a combat soldier as opposed to a specialist he will carry this out in his combat unit, and then spend the next two perfecting his skills, and the last handing his expertise over to his replacement. His noncoms are made up of approximately one third regulars and two thirds conscripts like himself, who have been selected for special training after their first few weeks service. His officers will be for the most part regulars, although a number will be university graduates who have qualified as reserve officers and are serving for one to three years. The regular officers will have served between three and six years at a military academy before being commissioned, and will receive further training at advanced academies and staff colleges as they proceed upwards through the ranks. Hand in hand with military training at all levels comes political indoctrination, and the Marxist-Leninist approach to solving military problems is an essential part of the soldier's training. Like every other aspect

Above: Warsaw Pact troops with SA-7 Grail surface-to-air missile launchers.
Right: Soviet soldiers in Afghanistan.
Below right: BTR-60Ps in typical attack formation.

of Soviet life, the armed forces are geared to 'norms'. Whether it be on the time to change a track on a BMP, the ability to put so many rounds of 122mm D-30 towed howitzer in target area per minute, or the correct setting up of a regimental command post, all are subject to strict laid down detailed standards, and every unit is plagued by a constant stream of inspectors, who have come to check whether it is achieving its norms.

In the past, two weaknesses of the Soviet Army have been made much of in Western writing. The first is the lack of initiative allowed at middle and lower levels. It has always been contended that the rigidity of the communist system would not countenance any deviation from the official line, and that this was reflected as much in the armed forces as any other sector of Soviet society. This, however, is no longer so. During the past decade, the Soviet High Command has realized that too much rigidity conflicts with the fast moving battle which it is intending to fight. The middle and junior commanders are therefore being encouraged to use their initiative very much more than hitherto, and this is likely to grow further in the years ahead. The other is the Soviet lack of experience in action since 1945, something which was a popular accusation in the late Sixties and early Seventies, when the US Army was experiencing much high intensity fighting in Southeast Asia. For a start, Afghanistan, with upwards of 120,000 Soviet soldiers being stationed there at any one time, is providing valuable operational experience. Furthermore, the Soviet missions to Third World countries often find themselves embroiled in local wars, which gives them not just experience, but also the chance to handle and evaluate Soviet

military equipment in active service conditions. Two prime examples are the campaign in the Ogaden between Ethiopia and Somalia in 1978, which produced important lessons in the value of heliborne operations, and the current situation in the Lebanon, where Soviet advisers in Syria are gaining particular experience in the effectiveness of their air defense systems.

How then is the Soviet soldier likely to fight in World War III? Like any conscript, he resents the

Above: Motor rifle troops attack supported by Mi-24 Hind-D attack helicopter.
Above right: Canadian infantry dismount from a Bell UH-1D.
Right: Soviet infantry suppress a strongpoint with AK-47 assault rifles and 30mm grenade launchers, supported by BMPs.

fact that he has to do military service and cannot wait to finish his term. He dislikes the comparative harshness and austerity under which he is made to live compared to his civilian life. He is bored by the

Above: Dutch YP-408 wheeled APCs.
Right: Canadian infantryman in Arctic combat kit. He has a Belgian 7.62mm FN rifle used by a number of European NATO armies.

amount of political indoctrination to which he is subjected, and particularly angry when it eats into what he regards as his very limited and precious free time. Nevertheless, he is well disciplined, tough and as well trained as he has ever been.

The quality of the armies of the other Warsaw Pact members is more questionable. Probably the best is that of the GDR, the most enthusiastic nation other than the Soviet Union about the Pact. Training and approach, as well as tactics, in the other armies mirror the Soviet Army, and much of the equipment used is Soviet, which gives the Pact a distinct advantage over NATO in terms of commonality of weapons systems. Nevertheless, there is a distinct political question mark on their will to fight. Apart from in the GDR, relations between Soviet troops stationed in Eastern Europe and the local populations are lukewarm at best. Indeed, the Soviet troops are allowed little contact with their 'hosts'. It may therefore be that the Soviet Union will not commit satellite armies to the offensive unless it is forced to do so. There is also the danger of unrest within Eastern Europe, which may force the USSR to keep troops stationed there.

NATO's main problem is lack of standardization. This is not just in equipment, but in tactics, organization and training. While the US, British and Canadian Armies are all-regular, the remainder are largely conscript, with varying terms of service. Thus while,

the German conscript serves for fifteen months, his Belgian counterpart, if posted to Germany, has only an eight month term. Within the Central Region, the two largest ground force contingents are those of the FRG and the USA.

The US Army went through a difficult period in the Seventies. Although Vietnam had given it extensive operational experience, much of it was not applicable to Europe and the emphasis in approach had to be radically changed. Vietnam had also been a chastening experience. The growing unpopularity of the war had isolated the US Armed Forces and morale suffered, and the incidence of drug taking and 'fragging' rose alarmingly. The decision to end conscription and move to a volunteer army also took time to implement, and the early volunteers were of low caliber. Budgetary restrictions meant cutbacks, and these together with the recession resulted in US servicemen abroad, especially in Germany, finding it difficult to make ends meet financially.

In the past few years there has been a radical change. The Army is obtaining a much higher quality of recruit and much effort has gone into improving terms and conditions of service. A further move to raise morale has been the introduction of a regimental system, whereby a soldier will serve as much as possible with one particular unit, on much the same lines as the British system. In addition, the Cohort Scheme provides for companies of recruits to do their basic training together and then be posted

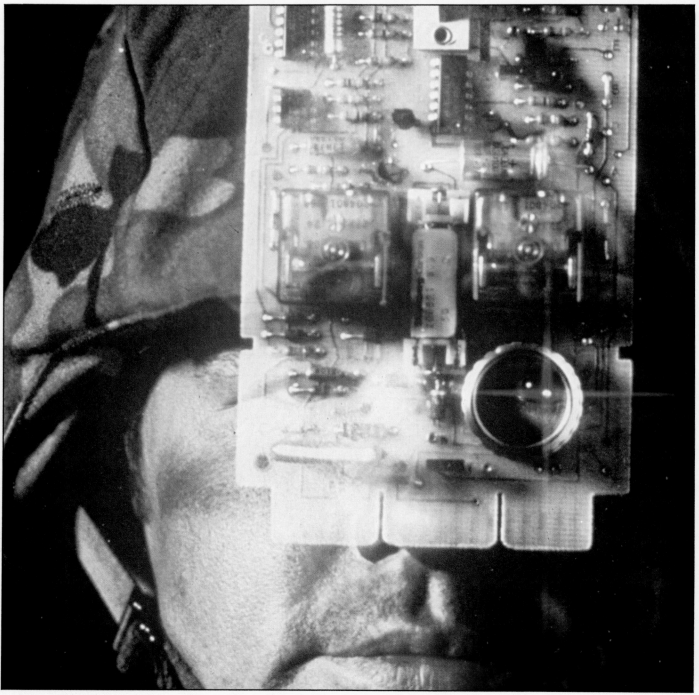

Top far left: US troops in Vietnam.
Top left: US infantryman with M-16 Armalite rifle.
Left: The modern combat soldier is becoming increasingly wedded to high technology.
Above: US soldier training with a laser fire simulator.
Below: Infrared goggles enable the soldier to see at night.

en bloc overseas, so that they will continue to soldier with one another. The adoption of the Airland concept as official doctrine has instilled the Army with a much more positive sense of purpose, and recent and ongoing equipment improvements are resulting in a more dynamic force.

The armed forces of the Federal Republic of Germany, the Bundeswehr, came into existence in 1955, when the FRG was made a member of NATO. With the spectre of the first half of the 20th Century there to haunt them, the government was determined that never again would the armed forces be allowed to dictate policy. Emphasis was therefore placed on the concept of the 'civilian in uniform', and the fact that the Bundeswehr was an entirely new force with no connection with its predecessor, the Wehrmacht. A further constitutional point is that the Bundeswehr is strictly for defense of the homeland and will never be operationally deployed outside the borders of the FRG in pursuit of national policy. With these restrictions it might seem that the result would be an ineffectual force, but this is not so. German soldiers have always been first class and, although they only serve for 15 months, they quickly reach a high standard of training, and are led by professional officers and senior noncoms. In terms of equipment, too, much of it is home produced and among the best in the world. Thus, although no serving German soldier has been tested in combat, there is little doubt that he will perform well, and will be well motivated in that he is defending his homeland.

The other two volunteer armies, those of the Canadians and British, are both very professional. Although the Canadian contribution to the Central Region is small, one brigade group, which is the CENTAG immediate reserve, it is nonetheless valuable for that. Canadian troops have also had much recent experience in peacekeeping operations overseas. The British Army, too, is finely honed. Continuing operational experience in Northern Ireland, although in many ways frustrating, does have one bonus in the valuable experience it gives to junior commanders, both officers and noncoms, and this was amply demonstrated in the 1982 Falklands Campaign. The latter also confirmed that British Army training in general was on the right lines and provided a useful operational evaluation of weapons systems.

The other NATO armies are all conscript. They also suffer from continuing budgetary problems, which makes the procurement of high technology weapons systems more and more of an uphill struggle. This is most marked on the Southern Flank, where Turkey, although a very loyal member of NATO, possesses an army with largely obsolescent equipment, but lacks the money to modernize on her own. The same, too, can be said for NATO's newest member, Spain. The other problem on the Southern Flank is Greece. Her continuing feud with Turkey over Cyprus does result in difficulties in cooperation between the two. Nevertheless, the will is there.

The problem of standardization of equipment is one with which NATO has grappled since its inception. The root of it lies in the fact that, being a democratic organization, its members are there largely for reasons of self interest. When it comes to weapons and equipment, there is an understandable concern to maintain national defense industries. Yet, there has been some progress, both in terms of collaborative projects and agreements such as that on the standard NATO small arms round, which is currently 7.62mm but is soon to change to 5.56mm. NATO, however, will never reach the level of standardization of the Warsaw Pact.

There is also independence of thought in tactical concepts. Thus, in the Central Region, while all national corps observe the policy of Forward Defense, there are different interpretations of it. While the Germans understandably obey it to the letter and will not give ground until forced to do so, the other national corps take a slightly more flexible approach. One other difficulty is over language, but this is also the same for the Warsaw Pact, where, although the official language is Russian, many of the Soviet recruits from the more farflung Soviet Socialist Republics cannot speak it. With NATO, the official language is English, and this is spoken at all integrated headquarters. Within the national corps, the national language is spoken, and with corps of different nations fighting side by side, the requirement for liaison officers who are bilingual becomes most

Left: US Dragon antitank guided weapon team.
Above: West German Cobra antitank guided missiles.

important. One area where standardization has made much progress within NATO is over staff procedures and the majority of operational procedures are now common for all member armies.

The disparate character of the NATO alliance is a disadvantage in some ways. Nevertheless, the solidarity of the member nations is in itself a deterrent, and coalition warfare has been successfully waged in the past. There is no reason to suppose that it will not be so in the future.

When considering the relative strengths between the two alliances, it is difficult to be precise in terms of numbers of men and weapons equipments. Indeed, estimates vary enormously. To give but one example, NATO believes that it is outnumbered by as much as 3:1 in tanks in the Central Region, whereas the Soviet Union will only admit to a very slight advantage in its favor, arguing that NATO estimates do not take into account those tanks in storage. Any figures thus given can only be approximations.

On the Northern Flank, the Soviet Union has two motor rifle divisions permanently stationed facing a single Norwegian brigade. In time of war, she could reinforce these with an additional seven divisions from Leningrad, which would give her a total of some 1700 tanks and 2000 artillery pieces and mortars. NATO meanwhile could field a total of some 13

infantry brigades, but these would be for the defense of not just Norway, but Denmark and Schleswig Holstein as well. In the Central Region, including indigenous forces based in national territory, but excluding those in North America, NATO has available some 39 divisions, with 7700 tanks and 4550 artillery/mortar pieces. Opposing these are 95 Warsaw Pact divisions with approximately 25,000 tanks and 17,500 artillery/mortar pieces. Eight divisions (1250 tanks, 1550 artillery/mortar pieces) in Italy face 17 divisions (4300 tanks and 2700 artillery/mortar pieces) in Hungary, while Greece and Turkey in Europe can muster 25 divisions (2900 tanks, 2850 artillery/mortar pieces) to oppose 33 Warsaw Pact divisions (6900 tanks, 5700 artillery/mortar pieces) in Bulgaria and Romania. Finally Turkey will have to defend her eastern border with the Soviet Union with 12 divisions (1000 tanks, 1800 artillery/mortar pieces) against 19 Soviet divisions (4100 tanks and 4000 artillery/mortar pieces).

It would seem, therefore, that NATO is seriously outnumbered on every front, but these bald figures do not give the complete picture. For a start, only those Soviet divisions stationed in other Warsaw Pact member states are maintained at close to established strength, along with her eight airborne divisions. Of the 67 divisions based in European USSR, about half are maintained at 70% strength, and could be brought up to full establishment in a few days. The remainder are kept at less than a third of established strength. These also could be fully mobilized within days. The remainder of the total standing force of some 175 divisions would, apart from those stationed on the Sino-Soviet border and in Afghanistan, take much longer to mobilize and would have obsolete equipment. Furthermore, there is the question of the reliability of the satellite armies. In particular, Romania, which has always taken a very independent line, might well decline to join in military action, which would remove her nine divisions from those facing Greece and Turkey.

NATO also has a number of its divisions and corps at less than full strength. While the US Army in Europe (USAREUR) requires four brigades and some individual reinforcements from CONUS, the frontline German corps are almost up to strength. 1(BR) Corps, however, relies on a full infantry division being deployed from the UK, and for unit reinforcements to bolster its three divisions in place in Germany. 1(BE) Corps relies on the third brigade of each of its two divisions being mobilized in time, and 1(NL) Corps has to mobilize one of its three divisions from scratch. However, the US Army could fly across a complete corps of three divisions, III(US) Corps from CONUS in a matter of days to reinforce the Central Region, and there is also France, whose strength has not been included in the calculations so far. Although, she is no longer part of the NATO military infrastructure, she has made it very clear that a Warsaw Pact invasion of the Central Region would be a direct threat to her and that she would give military support to NATO in that event. At present she is restructuring her forces to create a Rapid Action Force of one light armored division and four antitank infantry divisions with significant helicopter support, one of whose roles would be to provide indepth support to NATO forces. This would be a valuable addition.

If the Warsaw Pact intends to launch an attack against NATO territory, it must decide how much warning time it is prepared to give NATO of its intentions. The more divisions it mobilizes, the stronger its forces, but this will take time, and will be a major indicator to NATO. In turn, therefore, it will allow NATO to deploy more forces before hostilities break out, which will make the Warsaw Pact task that much more difficult. NATO planners are fully aware of this and consider that there are three possible scenarios.

Below: Infrared jammer on a UH-1H helicopter.
Bottom: British Scorpion light tanks firing by night.
Right: Canadian West German built Leopard 1.

In the first, which is currently seen as the most likely, there will be a period of growing tension, at some point during which the Warsaw Pact will begin to mobilize. NATO will do likewise, and the two alliances would sit and glower at one another. At this point the tension would cease rising and probably drop. After a period of time, NATO would withdraw most of its forces from their deployment positions, and it would be then that the Warsaw Pact would choose to invade. In other words, they would sacrifice strategic for tactical surprise. Alternatively, NATO might receive a seven day warning of the outbreak of hostilities. This would allow both sides just time enough to mobilize their first line reserves and deploy them. Finally, the third option is where the Soviets may decide to sacrifice force for surprise and initially use just those divisions in the GDR, Poland, Hungary and Czechoslovakia, which are, of course, virtually fully up to strength. In this event, NATO would receive as little as 48 hours warning, and, given this, the Soviets would catch the Alliance while it was still deploying, which, in itself, would be a force multiplier.

The next question is the means which NATO would have at its disposal in order to obtain warning of an impending attack. There are several. Some indication of Warsaw Pact intentions would probably be obtained from the political signalling during the period of tension. Warsaw Pact deployment is also likely to take place under the guise of field maneuvers. However, any NATO or Warsaw Pact exercise involving over 25,000 men in Europe must, as a result of the Helsinki agreements, be notified to the opposing alliance. Thus, large scale maneuvers by the Warsaw Pact in a period of political tension would be regarded with grave suspicion by NATO. If, however, the Warsaw Pact failed to inform NATO, there are other ways of detecting that they are taking place. One method would be through the US and British Military Missions to East Germany. It was originally agreed at Potsdam that the Soviets, British and Americans would exchange military missions within the zones of occupation in Germany. This has never been rescinded and, although both sides impose rigid restrictions on the activities of these missions, they do provide a very useful window into the enemy's camp. Information might also come from espionage, defectors or refugees.

There are, however, a number of surveillance devices which can be employed. Intelligence satellites (Intelsats) are being put up in increasing numbers by both the Soviets and Americans, and much intelligence can be gained from the pictures which they transmit back to earth. Many people believe that they are so effective that nothing can be hidden from them. This, however, is an exaggeration and they do have their drawbacks, and there have been many examples of this during the last decade. They failed to detect the

Egyptian preparations for crossing the Suez Canal in October 1973, and led to an incorrect estimate of the number of Cubans on the island of Grenada prior to the US invasion in the fall of 1983. These are but two incidents. Nevertheless, they are an invaluable intelligence tool. Coming closer to earth, there are the so called 'spy planes'. The Lockheed U-2 is still in service, and has now been joined by the TR-1, which is a derivative and very similar in configuration. The most outstanding, though, of this type of aircraft is the Lockheed SR-71 Blackbird. It can cruise at a speed of over 2000mph for over two hours at a height of 15 miles, and carries a long focus camera which can cover 125 miles of ground with one shot. It also has infrared (IR) cameras which can photograph through clouds, and sideways looking airborne radar (SLAR). The performance of the Blackbird is such that it can photograph an area half the size of Italy in one hour, and the resolution is such that, from ten miles up, a golf ball on the ground can be detected. SLAR is also carried by tactical reconnaissance aircraft, and has the great advantage that the aircraft can fly within friendly territory and detect what is happening behind the enemy's front lines. Another class of airborne surveillance devices are remotely piloted vehicles (RPV) and drones. Both the Warsaw Pact and NATO are making increasing use of these, and a classic example of their use was by the Israelis in the Lebanon in 1982 when they used RPVs to pinpoint Syrian air defense installations in the Bekaa Valley. Latest developments include remotely piloted helicopters (RPH). Up until now, however, RPVs and drones have flown photographic missions, and the prints have had to be developed on landing. The new systems will be designed to give real time intelligence, and a good example of this is the PAVE Tiger being developed by the US Air Force. Indeed, all surveillance systems, to be effective, will need this ability in the highly mobile battle of the future, especially if Airland 2000 is accepted as NATO doctrine.

A further intelligence source lies in the field of communications and electronics. Two forms of intelligence are involved here, communications intelligence (COMINT) and electronic intelligence (ELINT). COMINT involves the monitoring of radio nets, and much information can be picked up from them. In order to minimize this, communicators using insecure nets use special voice codes, but these can be often quickly broken. Also, voice nets down to battalion level are now usually secure. This is done by scrambling the speech as it passes through the transmitter. Nevertheless, the signal is still detectable, even though it is indecipherable, and radio direction finding (RDF) equipment can pinpoint its location. It is also possible by analysing the amount of signals traffic and knowing its location to work out what type of station it is – headquarters, logistic, artillery etc.

US Nike-Hercules air defense missile.

It is not, however, only radios which give out detectable signals, but radars as well, and they can also be pinpointed. Position finding of both radios and radars is known as ELINT.

ELINT and COMINT are but one weapon in the field of electronic warfare (EW) and are known as EW Support Measures (ESM) or Passive Electronic Countermeasures (ECM). A third measure which comes under this category is deception. Here, by sending out false information over the radio, especially on a known enemy frequency or spurious signals, the object is to confuse and misinform the enemy. There is also Active ECM, which takes the form of jamming of radio nets and radars and physical destruction. Jamming is a very effective method, especially against forward radio nets in a fast moving battle or air defense radars, and the destruction of headquarters and communication centers (commcens), having located them through RDF, could be carried out by artillery fire, air strike or special forces, leaving enemy forces without effective control.

C^3 is vital to the successful conduct of the modern battle, and both sides will strive to protect their systems against attack, electronic or physical. The methods they use to do this come under the broad heading of Electronic Counter Counter Measures (ECCM). The longer the transmission the more likely the transmitter will be located. Hence, one key to successful ECCM is to keep transmissions as short as possible. This can be done to an extent through good radio discipline, but modern radio design now has potential for what is known as 'burst transmis-

sion', where the transmission is sent out as a concentrated short, sharp burst. Another technical ploy is 'frequency hopping', where each transmission makes use of a number of frequencies. There are, however, problems with this. Firstly, the receiving stations must be matched in terms of frequencies with the transmitter, and this is complicated and expensive. Also, there are only a limited number of frequencies available within the various bands. Each radio net needs its own frequency if it is not to interfere with other nets, and there are problems enough as it is in providing sufficient frequencies for the large number of nets on the battlefield. Thus, if nets are to have multiple frequencies, the problem is made worse. In any event, most nets have a reserve frequency to be used in the event of prolonged jamming.

Headquarters are very vulnerable to physical destruction. Also, the higher the level of the HQ, the larger it is. Thus, while a battalion HQ consists of no more than five or six vehicles, that for a division will be ten times the size. Concealment, which is one means of protection, is therefore harder. Physical protection, in the form of making all HQ vehicles armored, also helps. Another form of this is putting the headquarters in cellars, or even building hardened bunkers in peacetime in which to house it. The other form of protection is never to stay too long in the same location. As a normal rule, HQs will move at least once every 24 hours, and always have an alternate HQ or 'step up', which can take over if the main HQ is moving or attacked.

The electronic battle is just as important as the fire fight, and the measures being employed in it are becoming ever more sophisticated.

Deterrent or threat? A nuclear weapon explosion.

3. NUCLEAR, CHEMICAL AND BIOLOGICAL

The most awesome aspect of World War III is the very real possibility that nuclear, chemical and even biological (NBC) weapons might be employed. These threaten the very continued existence of the human race. Yet, paradoxically, their very existence has been a major reason why World War III has not so far broken out. Indeed, their very awfulness has been and is a very effective deterrent.

NATO still holds to the doctrine of Flexible Response, which was described in Chapter One, while the Warsaw Pact believes in the ability to win a war fought at any level. Up until now, NATO has viewed tactical nuclear weapons as a force multiplier and has believed that selective use of them would make the Russians stop and reconsider. The Soviets, however, have a different perspective. If they are to overrun Western Europe, they must also concern themselves with the strategic nuclear threat from CONUS. Furthermore, they do not believe that it is possible to fight a limited nuclear war. On the other hand, although the Soviets have made a 'no first use' declaration, it is quite possible that they might well seriously consider the use of tactical nuclear weapons if their offensive had become bogged down, or if they thought that NATO was about to use them. One of their key initial objectives, however, is the identifica-

tion and destruction of NATO tactical nuclear weapon sites, and failure to achieve this might also tempt them into a nuclear strike. Nevertheless, within NATO circles there are increasing doubts as to the relevance of the tactical nuclear weapon, and in the future, less reliance is likely to be placed on it. It is, however, very unlikely that it will vanish from the battlefield, especially as long as the Warsaw Pact possesses it, and the prospect of the nuclear battlefield remains.

There are three basic categories of nuclear weapon, although the boundaries between them are difficult to define precisely. Strategic systems, which are outside the scope of this book, refer to intercontinental systems, land, air or sea-launched. These launch media are generally referred to as the 'nuclear triad'. They have a very high yield, and examples are the US Minuteman and Trident and the Soviet SS-18 and SS-19. The next category are known as theater nuclear weapons. These are limited by range to particular theaters of operations, ie Europe. It is over these that the current nuclear debate is focussed. When the Russians began to deploy the SS-20, a mobile rocket system with a range of almost 3000 miles, west of the Urals in the mid-Seventies, NATO became increasingly concerned. The existing Per-

shing Is had a much smaller yield in comparison and only had a range of 500 miles. The only other weapon that they had which could match it without using strategic weapons was aerial delivery, using the General Dynamics FB-111. The decision was therefore taken in 1979 to modernize the theater nuclear forces (TNF) in Europe by deploying Pershing II, with over double the range of its predecessor, and the Cruise system, a very accurate weapon with a range of 1700 miles, which is designed to fly at low level in order to avoid radar defenses. It is an ideal weapon against fixed targets, but its slow speed means that it is not suitable against mobile targets. The Soviets see this deployment as a very grave threat and, in retaliation, are now deploying theater systems in the satellite countries. An offer by the US not to deploy Cruise and Pershing if the Soviets would dismantle their SS-20s was not taken up. However, these systems are more likely to be used against strategic targets in Europe such as seats of government.

Tactical nuclear weapons are, on the other hand, very much part of the land battlefield. They are low yield with ranges limited to less than one hundred miles. NATO has two missile systems which it uses in this role, Lance and Honest John, while the Warsaw Pact equivalents are the FROG and SCUD

Far left: US FB-111 bomber launching Short Range Attack Missile (SRAM) which carries a 200KT warhead 100 miles.
Left: Soviet SCUD-B tactical nuclear missiles with a range of some 150 miles.
Below: Soviet FROG-7 with a range of 40 miles.

49

series. There are also nuclear shells which can be fired from conventional artillery guns, and NATO uses the M110 203mm self-propelled howitzer for this, as well as in conventional roles.

There are five major effects of nuclear weapons – heat, blast, immediate and residual radiation, and electromagnetic pulse (EMP). The core of a nuclear explosion is at a very high temperature, which can be measured in millions of degrees centigrade. Thermal radiation being emitted by the core causes a fireball around it, and this produces dazzle and heat effects. Dazzle caused by the brightness of the burst can produce temporary blindness, and a few might suffer retinal burns if their eyes were focussed directly on the explosion. The thermal effects are caused by flash and flame. Flash causes first and second degree burns to exposed skin, and will set clothing, dry grass and undergrowth alight within a certain range of the

explosion. The smaller the yield, the more likely that these effects will be felt, since the thermal radiation arrives more quickly and produces a sharper temperature rise. Blast consists of a shock wave caused by the explosion, and a wind which follows closely behind it. While the former will blow objects in its path down, and be reflected if they are solid, the wind produces a drag effect.

Radiation exists in four forms – alpha, beta, gamma and neutron. Alpha and beta particles have little penetrating power, although the former can cause damage to human tissue if inhaled or absorbed through an open wound. Neither is of much military significance. Gamma and neutron particles are, however, highly penetrative, and it is from them that most casualties are caused. They attack the body cells, and bone marrow, which produces new blood cells, and the lining of the intestine and brain and

Previous page: Multiple Launch Rocket System (MLRS) in action. This can be used to deliver chemical warheads.
Left: Setting up a SCUD launch position.
Above: SS-21 launcher vehicle. SS-21 is to replace FROG in Soviet use.

muscle cells are also particularly susceptible. The amount of damage caused to the individual is dependent on the dose received, and is measured in terms of rads. By way of example, a dose of up to 150 rads will cause no immediate effects, while between 150 and 250 rads will result in nausea and vomiting within 24 hours, but recovery within 48 hours. A 250–350 rad dose brings about nausea and vomiting within four hours, and then the patient will appear to recover. However, the symptoms will then reappear leading to some deaths within two to four weeks. 350–600 rads produces the initial symptoms within two hours and prolonged incapacity. Half of those exposed to a 450 rad dose will die within two to four weeks. Over 600 rads results in almost 100% deaths in one week, while 3000 causes total incapacitation within one hour. Neutron radiation is more complex because, unlike gamma particles which react with the electrons in the atoms of the target, it reacts with the nuclei of these atoms. It can either bounce off, thereby displacing the atom, or be absorbed by the nucleus, which will result in the emission of gamma radiation. Ionization is likely to be caused and this will effect the electrical properties of the target.

Immediate radiation is that which is emitted within one minute of the burst, and will result in neutron and gamma radiation, with the former traveling very much faster than the latter. In order to give some idea of the results of immediate radiation, an individual unprotected at 1000 yards from a 20 kiloton (KT) burst could expect to receive 3000 rads in ten seconds. Residual radiation, on the other hand, is mainly made up of gamma and beta radiation, and is spread either through neutron induced activity (NIA) or fallout. NIA means that all material close to the burst is bombarded by neutrons which may react with the nuclei of some of the target atoms to produce radioactive isotopes, while fallout represents the radioactive material which falls to earth, and will be carried by the prevailing winds. Both types of residual radiation do decay, and as a very rough rule, what is known as the Seven and Ten Law is applied. If the time after the burst is multiplied by seven, the dose rate is divided by ten. Thus, if the dose rate is 1000 rads per hour one hour after the explosion, it will drop to 100 rads per hour six hours later.

The electromagnetic effects of a nuclear explosion are often ignored, but are very significant. They come in two forms. Firstly, there is the emission of a pulse of electromagnetic (EMP) radiation, and then there are changes in the electromagnetic characteristics of the atmosphere due to ionizing radiation from the explosion and fallout, together with an excess of vapor. While the first can cause direct damage to electrical and radio equipment, the latter brings about a radar and radio blackout or propagation problems which can last for several hours. In particular EMP can cause insulation failures in cables, the tripping of relays and circuit breakers by excessive induced voltages, direct damage to signal equipment and items which contain magnetics can be upset by induced magnetic fields. As for the ionization aspect, it is High Frequency (HF) radios and radars which will be the most affected. Such a possible breakdown in communications and surveillance equipment could be very damaging.

The degree of these effects is dependent not only on the size of the nuclear warhead and the distance away from the explosion, but also on the height of the burst above ground. This is defined as high or low airburst, surface and subsurface burst. A high air-

Left: A US Pershing 2 being fired. Now being deployed to Europe it can carry a 200KT warhead 1000 miles.
Above: A US 203mm M110 self-propelled howitzer which can fire small yield nuclear and chemical warheads.

burst is ideal for 'soft' targets, like men in the open, and will also produce the most effective disruption of long range radio communications. A low airburst, on the other hand, probably produces the best balance of effects against the majority of targets likely to be found on the battlefield, but each separate weapon yield has its own optimum height of burst for producing the maximum casualties and damage, and these are laid out in tables. A surface burst, where the fireball actually touches the ground, is known as a 'dirty' explosion because of the large amounts of fall out which it produces. It would only be used against very hard targets or to contaminate a very large area, and is unlikely to be used on the battlefield. Sub surface bursts are used in atomic demolition mines (ADM) as a means of causing extensive demolitions, but this form of tactical nuclear weapon is now being phased out.

A 15 KT airburst would produce the following approximate affects to men in certain situations within certain radii of the burst, or what is known as Ground Zero (GZ):

a. Men, unwarned and unprotected except by normal combat clothing could expect to be decapacitated by blast and radiation within 1050m of GZ and suffer second degree burns within 1400m.
b. If they are in slit trenches with some overhead cover, they will not be affected by thermal effects, but will suffer badly from radiation within 800m and blast within 400m.
c. If they are in armored personnel carriers (APC), blast will cause casualties to them and their vehicles within 600m and radiation within 950m.
d. In main battle tanks they will survive blast above 500m from GZ and radiation above 750m.

From this it will be seen that a measure of protection against nuclear weapons is possible.

Individual protection comes from a sound knowledge of the immediate action drills and the wearing of protective clothing. If a nuclear burst is spotted, the immediate action is to close the eyes to protect them from the flash and go to ground, covering all exposed parts of the body, and to remain there until the shock wave and wind have passed. Radiation is guarded against by the wearing of respirators and

NBC clothing. All Warsaw Pact and NATO armies are equipped with this, and do much of their training wearing it. In terms of comfort, NATO has the edge over its potential adversary, who uses suits, overboots and gloves made of a rubberized material, which is comparatively bulky and very uncomfortable to wear for a long period, especially when the weather is hot. NATO armies have long used clothing made up of charcoal-based materials, which is much lighter than the Warsaw Pact equivalent. Nevertheless, eating, drinking and other bodily functions in a contaminated area are very difficult to carry out, and some are impossible to do without being contaminated. A more satisfactory way of enduring the nuclear battlefield is by collective protection. Almost all armored fighting vehicles (AFV) are equipped with what is called NBC protection, which means creating an NBC free atmosphere within the vehicle. This is done by sealing the crew compartment, both physically and by creating an air overpressure inside, with air from the outside being passed through charcoal filters in order to decontaminate it. Another form of collective protection is the construction of shelters with sufficient overhead earth cover. Thus, a shelter with three feet of overhead earth cover will give the individuals inside more than ten times the level of protection against residual radiation that of those in a main battle tank, and two hundred times

Above and right: US soldiers operating in a simulated chemical environment. They are not wearing protective gloves which makes them vulnerable to most forms of chemical attack.

that of an unprotected man in the open.

Nevertheless, soldiers are going to have to fight on a contaminated battlefield without the advantage of collective protection, and it is most important that commanders constantly monitor individual radiation levels. For this, personal dosimeters are provided and the latest British example is worn like a watch on the wrist. The commander checks it with another instrument which gives a read out in rads, and from this he can determine the radiation status of his unit. Once a unit has reached a certain radiation level, usually 150 rads, they should be withdrawn to a decontaminated area, but must, before anything else, decontaminate themselves. This normally takes the form of hosing down with water and detergent.

It is also important to know precisely the extent of a contaminated area. After the burst, it is possible to be able to predict the rate and area of contamination by residual radiation if Ground Zero, the speed and direction of the wind, height and time of burst are known, as well as a rough idea of the yield. This will enable troops in that area to receive warning and prepare themselves. However, this must be confirmed later by radiation survey and constantly monitored.

Although neither side will be likely to use nuclear weapons at the outset of hostilities, nuclear planning will be carried out and is a constant process. There will be a continuous updating of information on targets. Both sides will be looking especially for concentrations of troops to make a worthwhile target, and indeed one of the commander's major problems is in trying to achieve the right balance between sufficient concentration to make a conventional attack and defend against it, and dispersing his troops so as not to make an obvious nuclear target. Target location, type, size and shape are particularly important aspects. At the same time, nuclear planning staffs must be aware of the positions of friendly troops, their radiation states and level of protection, as well as the direction of the wind. They will also need from the commander, guidance on the level of damage required, the acceptable risk to own troops and any particular limiting requirements. Knowing what nuclear weapons and warheads they have available, they can then select the most suitable system for the target and determine the required height of burst, ground zero and the time of burst, as well as predicted coverage. As a basic rule, the minimum yield available which will give adequate target coverage is selected. If nuclear release is then given, it is important to warn friendly troops in the area so that they can take precautions, but this must not be

done too soon as the enemy is also likely to be warned. Once, however, the first tactical nuclear weapon has been exploded on the battlefield, it is hard to predict the course that the war will take from then onwards.

Chemical warfare first made its presence felt during World War I, and is estimated to have caused over one million immediate and delayed casualties. Such was the revulsion against it, that all the major powers signed the 1925 Geneva Protocol banning its use, but the Soviet Union and US only interpret the Protocol as banning first use, and reserve the right to use it in retaliation. Between the wars there was evidence that the Japanese employed chemical warfare in China, and the Italians used it in Ethiopia. It was, not, however, used in World War II, although both the Allies and Germans had extensive chemical stocks. Since World War II, the US employed a form of chemical warfare in their jungle defoliation operations in Vietnam, using Agent Orange, a herbicide containing a lethal compound called dioxin. There have also been accusations that the Vietnamese have used Soviet made chemicals in South East Asia, and that the Soviets have employed them in Afghanistan. These are the so called 'yellow rain' weapons. It is fact, however, that both the Soviet Union and US possess large stocks of chemical weapons. The Americans have not added to theirs since 1969, but now appear, in the face of the Soviet chemical threat,

to be beginning to modernize their stocks. Furthermore, Soviet military doctrine regards chemical warfare as part of conventional war, and it is very likely that she will employ it from the outset.

Chemical agents are divided into two broad types, persistent and non-persistent, lethal and incapacitating. The main lethal agents used are known as nerve agents because they attack the nervous system. The two most well known were developed by the Germans during World War II, and are tabun and sarin, which are respectively coded GA and GB, and are known as G agents, while a postwar development, VX, which is now the most common of the nerve agents, is known as a V agent. The early symptoms of nerve agents are running nose and excess of saliva, tightness in the chest, pinpointing of the pupils, blurred vision, and muscle twitching if the agent has entered through the skin. These will grow more severe, and be joined by headaches, drooling, excessive sweating, dizziness and general weakness. Finally nausea and vomiting will be induced, along with involuntary defecation and urination, muscle twitching and jerking, and eventually breathing will stop. G agents appear in the form of a vapor and are relatively non-persistent, while V agents are non-volatile highly oily liquids, and very persistent.

Blister agents include one of the original World War I agents, mustard gas, now known as HD. While nerve agents incapacitate and cause death quickly, blister agents act much more slowly. The initial symptoms will be irritation in the eyes, burning and reddening of the skin and, if inhaled, a burning sensation in the throat, accompanied by hoarseness and fever. Blisters will then develop, causing blindness and more fatally will attack the lungs. They appear either as a heavy vapor or liquid and are fairly persistent. Blood agents cause death by attacking the enzyme in the red blood cell which is responsible for removing carbon dioxide from the body. The victim will initially feel irritation in his eyes, nose, mouth and throat, accompanied by growing dizziness, nausea, headache, difficulty in breathing and, eventually, unconsciousness leading to death. AC (hydrogen cyanide) and CK (cyanogen chloride) are examples and were again developed during World War I. They are found in the form of a non-persistent vapor. The final category of lethal agents are known as choking agents, of which phosgene (CG) is perhaps the most well known. This attacks the lungs and brings about shortness of breath, choking and coughing, as well as general weakness. Death is brought about by the lungs flooding and usually occurs within about three hours. Choking agents are non-persistent.

Previous page: US soldiers on NBC training.
Left: German NBC clothing. Note special overboot on right foot.
Right: A Soviet soldier decontaminates a BRDM scout vehicle.

Above: US GIs in NBC clothing.
Below: US 203mm gun and the immediate effect of the nuclear round it has just fired.

Right: Soviet NBC survey team in action. The man in front is measuring radiation levels. Contaminated areas are usually marked on the ground.

Incapacitating agents are designed to make personnel militarily ineffective for varying lengths of time, and are not lethal. Thus, it could be argued that they fall outside the Geneva Protocol. Certainly, the Soviet Union is known to take a great interest in them, and they are the most likely type of chemical weapon which they will initially employ in World War III. The most effective of the decapacitating agents are known as physiochemical agents which act on the brain and central nervous system. Typical symptoms are confusion, distortion of vision, hallucinations, fear and anxiety, uncontrollable laughter, inertia and apathy and schizophrenia. A typical example is the drug LSD. They cannot be detected by the senses, unlike the lethal agents, but tend to be slow acting, can be unpredictable and can cause permanent psychotic disorders. The most common type of decapacitant, and one which has been frequently used, is the Riot Control agent, of which the most well-known examples are CS and VN gas. They cause a burning feeling in the eyes, as well as streaming tears, difficulty in breathing, coughing and tightness in the chest. However, against an enemy well trained and equipped in NBC protective measures, they are unlikely to be effective, and indeed, apart from being used to quell civil disturbances, are an ideal medium for chemical warfare training.

Chemical agents can be delivered in a number of ways. During World War I the main means was the artillery gas shell, and this is still in use. Mortars and rockets, especially multi-barrelled rocket launchers are other methods, as well as chemical land mines. Chemical agents can also be delivered from aircraft, in the form of sprays, bombs or bomblets.

As protection against chemical attack, troops are likely to wear NBC suits, with their respirators close at hand from the moment that hostilities break out. They will also have detector papers attached to their suits which will change color if chemicals are present. NBC sentries will be posted, with particular instructions to look out for low flying aircraft, to be suspicious of any form of bombardment and mist and smoke. Apart from the decapacitating agents, chemical agents do have distinctive smells. Choking agents have an odour of new mown hay, while blood agents are like bitter almonds. If a chemical attack is detected, the NBC sentry will sound the alarm, which in NATO is the banging together of two metal objects. Everyone in the area would then immediately mask up, and tests would be carried out to detect the type of agent being employed. This is important, since the first aid given is different for each. Nerve agents have chemical antidotes. In the British service, troops take oxime tablets, one every six hours, if a nerve agent attack is thought likely, and if they have been affected by it, they inject themselves with atrophine sulphate, using a high speed automatic hypodermic needle, which will act through NBC clothing. Oximes, however, can have undesirable side effects, and both the US and the British are currently developing new antidotes, which are likely to be in the form of a pyridostigmine tablet, taken every eight hours. Blood agents are countered by giving artificial respiration, but this should not be done for choking agents. Blister agents, are treated by washing out the eyes, and applying dry dressings to the blisters, which should not be burst. As for decapacitating agents, victims of psychochemical attack should be allowed to rest and sleep, but need to be under close supervision. As with nuclear radiation contamination, areas which have been subjected to chemical attack must, if a persistent agent has been used, be surveyed and marked.

In terms of chemical warfare planning, wind direction, as in nuclear planning, is an important factor, but so is the temperature gradient, which is the variation between temperatures taken just above the ground and at greater heights. Three conditions are defined – inversion, lapse and neutral. Inversion is when atmospheric conditions are stable, and temperature increases uniformly with height. With no turbulence and convection currents present, inversion produces the ideal situation for the use of chemical weapons. Lapse, on the other hand, is the least favorable condition. Here the air temperature decreases with height, and the atmospheric conditions are unstable, with no guarantee that the chemical might not blow back in the faces of friendly troops. This state normally exists on clear days with light winds. The neutral state lies in between the other two. Temperature remains roughly constant with increasing height, and it normally occurs on heavily overcast days. With meteorological information, it is, as with nuclear fallout, possible to predict chemically contaminated areas.

Chemical warfare will almost certainly be employed during World War III. Generally, non-persistent agents will be used, since contaminated areas are likely to inconvenience the user almost as much as the recipient. Furthermore, it is psychochemical agents which will be the most widespread, because of their obvious advantages.

In 1972 the major powers signed a Geneva convention prohibiting biological weapons and their stockpiling. Any party, however, may withdraw having given six months notice, and no provision was made for verification and inspection. Indeed, efforts to agree a similar ban on chemical weapons have stumbled on the last two points. A biological agent is a micro-organism which causes disease in man, plants or animals or deterioration in material. The micro-organisms themselves are grouped into fungi, protozoa, bacteria, rickettsiae and viruses. During World War II the Japanese employed biological warfare in China, and also carried out human experimentation at a research station which they set up at Harbin in Manchuria. There is also evidence that the partisans – Russian, Polish and Yugoslav – used it.

As far as the land battle is concerned, it is only the use of biological agents against personnel, which is relevant. There are two methods of delivery, either direct or through a vector, which is an animal or insect which transmits the disease. Thus, the mosquito is the vector for the transmission of yellow fever. On the battlefield, however, if biological agents are to be effective, they must act quickly and cause sufficient casualties, and therefore the direct method is preferred, using bomblets or sprays. The problem is that most diseases have a relatively long incubation period, which makes them unsuitable for battlefield use. While those which cause epidemics are likely to rebound on the user. Thus, up until now, they have never been considered as a suitable battlefied weapon.

Nevertheless, advances in the field of biotechnology are growing rapidly, and the boundaries between chemical and biological agents are becoming blurred. The traditional basic difference between the two, that one is manufactured in the laboratory while the other exists naturally, is now no longer so, in that biological agents can be produced artificially, and there is the prospect of as yet unknown powerful and virulent diseases being developed. The problem of the indiscrimination of such weapons, however, remains, although there are agents available which are non-transmissible or are self-limiting. While they are not suitable for the battlefield *per se*, against individuals or small groups they are very effective. A classic case of this was the assassination of the Bulgarian defector Georgi Markov in London in September 1978. The method of attack used was an airgun disguised as an umbrella, and a pellet containing a toxin penetrated into his blood stream. It is therefore possible that biological targets would more likely be senior commanders or headquarters, with attacks on them being made by covert groups.

Nuclear and chemical warfare are a very real threat in World War III, especially the latter. Biological weapons, on the other hand, are not likely to be used as a weapon of mass destruction on the battlefield, but could be used in a covert manner against small and vital targets.

Below: Soviet troops undergoing personal decontamination. Only once their protective clothing is 'clean' will they be able to remove it.

4. ARMOR

The division is not the only level at which reconnaissance elements are found in Warsaw Pact armies. At regimental level there is a reconnaissance company of 4 BMP and 6 BRDM, whose tasks are mainly engineer and chemical reconnaissance. There are also elements found at army level, and these will be used to cover the gaps between the divisional reconnaissance battalions.

Within the concept of Forward Defense, the task of NATO reconnaissance units is to identify the enemy's main axes of advance as quickly as possible, and also to destroy his reconnaissance elements before they come up against the main defensive position. Organizations and vehicles do, however, vary considerably between the nations involved.

The US is currently restructuring its organizations to reflect both the Airland Battle doctrine and the arrival of new equipment, especially the M1 Abrams main battle tank, and the M2/3 Bradley infantry fighting vehicle (IFV). The new divisional organization is known as 'Division 86', and has as its reconnaissance element an armored cavalry squadron of two armored cavalry troops and one air cavalry troop. The former each consist of sixteen M3 Bradleys organized into platoons, with two more at troop HQ. The air cavalry troop has three platoons –

Left: Two views of the Bradley M2/3.
Below: Soviet reconnaissance patrol with motorcycle combination and BRDM.

aeroweapons (nine attack helicopters), aeroscout (nine observation helicopters) and aerorifle (eight utility helicopters). The M3 Bradley is known as the Cavalry Fighting Vehicle (CFV) and has a five man crew. It is armed with the Hughes TOW antitank guided weapon (ATGW), with twin launcher tubes, a 25mm rapid fire cannon and a 7.62mm coaxial machine gun. Apart from integrating aerial reconnaissance with ground at divisional level, the US Army also differs from those of the Warsaw Pact in that there is a reconnaissance element at battalion level, both armor and mechanized infantry. This is known as the Scout Platoon and has six M3 Bradleys.

The West German reconnaissance vehicle is the SPPZ2 Luchs (Lynx). This is a large eight-wheeled vehicle, and owes its ancestry to the World War II Puma armored car. It is found at divisional reconnaissance level, and is organized into a battalion of 17 light reconnaissance patrols, each having two vehicles. The debate as to whether tracks or wheels are better for reconnaissance is a finely balanced one. Wheels mean a quieter vehicle, which is better for reconnaissance 'by stealth' and maintenance is also easier. However, tracks provide better cross-country performance. Nevertheless, with drive on all eight wheels, Luchs is highly mobile, but is rather large for this role. It is also somewhat lacking in fire power, with only a 20mm cannon and 7.62mm machine gun as armament. The Germans do not have reconnais-

sance elements at battalion level, but each brigade has a scout platoon, also equipped with Lynx.

The British, like the Americans, currently favor tracks for reconnaissance, although they do have some wheeled reconnaissance vehicles. The Combat Vehicle Reconnaissance (Tracked) [CVR(T)] family provides the basis, notably the Scorpion and Scimitar, both of which performed excellently in the Falklands campaign. Each of the three armored divisions in Germany has a medium reconnaissance regiment equipped with three squadrons of Scorpion, which mounts a 76mm gun. Each squadron has four troops of four Scorpions each, and also a surveillance troop with another member of the CVR(T) family, the Spartan APC. Five of these are in the troop and equipped with the ZB298 radar. Again like the US, the British have reconnaissance platoons with their armored and mechanized infantry battalions, and here the Scimitar, with the 30mm quick firing Rarden gun is used, six being in the platoon. The Belgians also use CVR(T) and indeed produce them jointly with the British. As for wheeled reconnaissance, the British Army uses the CVR(Wheeled) Fox, which also mounts a 30mm Rarden gun, and is found in the reconnaissance regiments of the 2nd Infantry Division, which reinforces 1(BR) Corps from the UK in time of war, and is responsible for the security of the Corps rear area.

If a Warsaw Pact attack in the Central Region is impending, NATO divisional reconnaissance elements will deploy right forward to the border and take up a line of observation. Initially, in front of them will be the FRG Border Police, who are responsible for the borders with the GDR and Czechoslovakia in peacetime, but they will probably withdraw before the Warsaw Pact actually crosses the border. It will be the task of the reconnaissance forces to try and prevent Warsaw Pact reconnaissance elements from penetrating. As the pressure builds up in front of the line of observation, so it will gradually pull back, imposing as much delay as its limited armament will allow, although it will be supported by attack helicopters and artillery. It is vital, though, that during this period it does not lose contact with the enemy, and the information which it passes back should be sufficient, along with other intelligence sources, to enable commanders to decide where the main thrusts are likely to occur, and to plan accordingly. Once the line has almost reached the main position, it will 'break clean' and move back to the rear to refurbish. The task of NATO reconnaissance troops will, however, have by no means finished. They are ideally organized to provide a quick reaction force to deal with airborne and heliborne landings, provide route security, NBC reconnaissance, traffic control and many other tasks.

Reconnaissance is an art calling for special skills in the soldier. He must be quick thinking and intelligent, used to using his own initiative and flexible in his approach. He must have the fieldcraft and cunning of a poacher. If he is effective in all this, he can play a vital part in the battle.

The main characteristics of the AFV are firepower, mobility, protection and flexibility. The task of the designer is to evolve the best balance between

them in order to best suit the role of the particular vehicle. Nowhere is this more difficult to achieve than with the main battle tank (MBT). Its two main tasks on the battlefield are the destruction of enemy armor and infantry support, and the tank is also used for shock action, hitting the enemy unexpectedly and catching him off balance. In definition it is a mobile gun platform and ideally needs to be hard hitting, highly mobile and well protected. While all tank producing nations agree that firepower is the most important characteristic, there is much debate over protection and mobility. The more protection in

Left: British Army Scimitar with 30mm Rarden gun.
Below: Soviet T-62s in typical attack formation.
Bottom: T-55s show their paces in soft going.

73

The US Army's Main Battle Tank – the M-1 Abrams.

Wind Sen

Commander's Ha

Commander's 0.5in M/G

Commander's S

Commander's Sight

Turret Controller
with Override

Smoke Grenade Launcher

Gunner's Primary Sight
& Laser Rangefinder

Auxiliary Telescope

Co-Axial 7.62mm M/Gun

105mm Cannon

Muzzle Reference Sensor

Driver's Control Box

Steering Yoke with Twistgrip Throttles

Forward Bulkhead

Brake Pedal

Forward Fuel Compartments

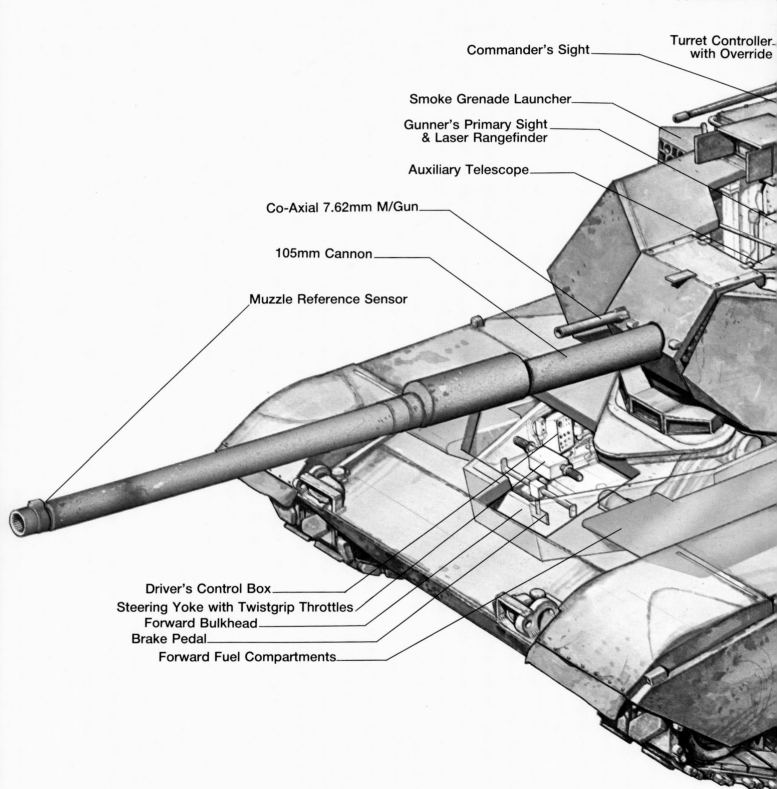

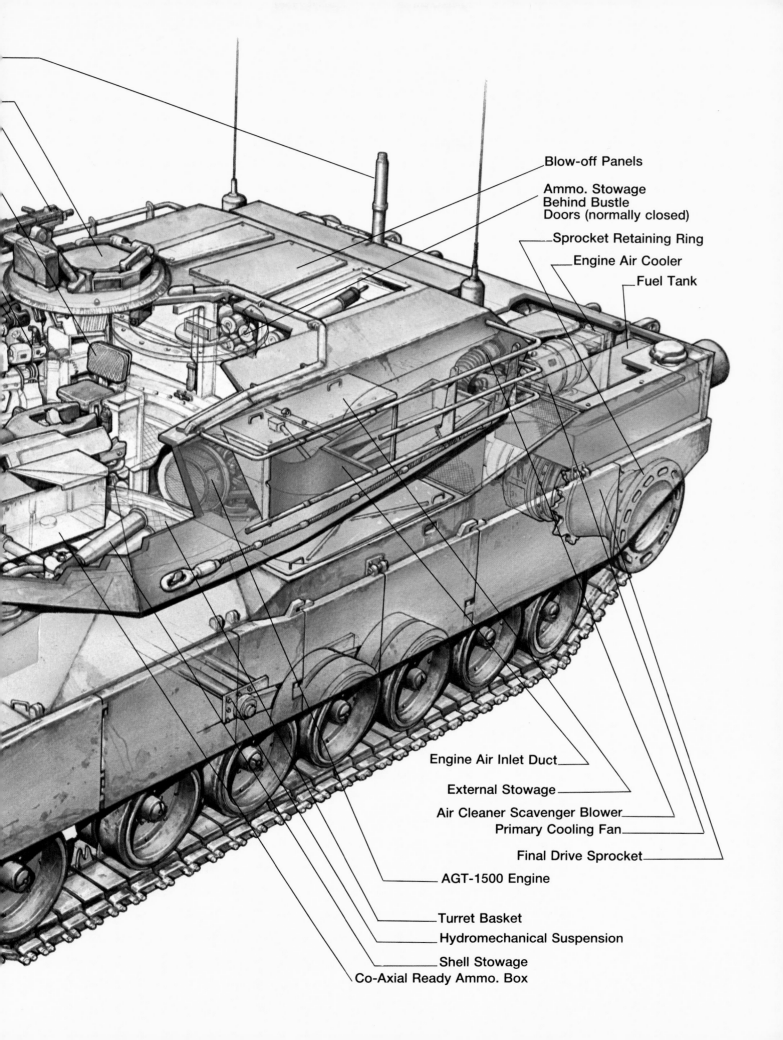

Blow-off Panels

Ammo. Stowage
Behind Bustle
Doors (normally closed)

Sprocket Retaining Ring

Engine Air Cooler

Fuel Tank

Engine Air Inlet Duct

External Stowage

Air Cleaner Scavenger Blower

Primary Cooling Fan

Final Drive Sprocket

AGT-1500 Engine

Turret Basket

Hydromechanical Suspension

Shell Stowage

Co-Axial Ready Ammo. Box

Above: Latest model of T-72 with modified turret. Known as M1980 or T-80.
Below: Basic T-72, which lacks grenade dischargers on turret front.
Right: T-64s, with which GSFG is equipped.

terms of armor given to a tank, the bulkier and more cumbersome it will be. Conversely, for a tank to be fast and highly mobile, it can only be lightly armored. Traditionally, the US and the Germans have always considered mobility to be the more important, while the British and Soviets prefer protection. The latter also believe that this is enhanced by giving the tank as low a silhouette as possible, but this means very cramped crew conditions, and indeed there is a maximum height for Warsaw Pact tankers.

The tanks in service, or coming into service today, represent, in the eyes of some pundits, the last of the heavy breed. They believe, and there is much in what they say, that the ever growing multiplicity of threats to the tank and its present size make it very vulnerable on the modern battlefield, and that tanks of the future will be very much smaller. They will make use of externally mounted guns, with the crew being housed in the hull rather than a turret. Their small size and agility will make them very much better protected than now, but just as effective. This new generation, however, is unlikely to be seen much before the turn of the century, and for World War III

it is the current generation which is of more concern.

The main two tanks in service with the Warsaw Pact today are the T-64 and T-72, which came into service at the beginning of the Seventies. There are, however, still a large number of older T-62s about, as well as some T-54/55s. The Soviets do not believe in discarding weapons systems unless they have to, and many of the divisions which are only at cadre strength in peacetime will be equipped with the older models in time of war. All the satellite armies are equipped with Soviet tanks. The main NATO tanks are the US M1 Abrams and M60, which will eventually be entirely replaced by the former, the German Leopard 1 and Leopard 2, and the British Chieftain and Challenger. Earlier US and British models, notably the M48 and Centurion, are still to be seen in some NATO armies.

In terms of tank guns, the NATO 105mm gun has now given way to the 120mm, while the Soviets have dispensed with the 115mm on T-62 for the 125mm on the two later models. There is also a marked move away by both sides from the traditional rifled gun to the smoothbore. In the past rifling was

77

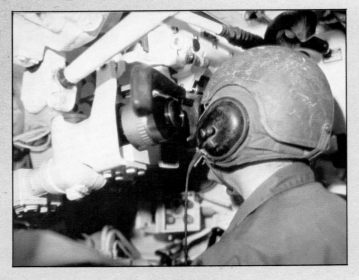

Above: US M60A3 gunner looking through his sights.
Above right: Leopard 2 with its 120mm smoothbore gun.
Right: Leopard 1 firing its 105mm gun.
Below: The US M60, which will be replaced by the M1 Abrams in time.

considered necessary in order to impart accuracy. The penalties are, however, that the barrel wears out relatively quickly. Also, the hotter the propellant charge, the higher the muzzle velocity of the round, which means improved accuracy and greater range, but also increases wear to the rifling, which degrades accuracy. A smoothbore gun, does not suffer this limitation, but accuracy has to be enhanced in another way, and this is done by using fin stabilized projectiles, which are, however, much more expensive than the conventional projectile. Nevertheless, the Soviet 125mm gun is smoothbore, as is the 120mm on Leopard 2. The US is also about to replace the rifled 105mm on the Abrams with the latter. The next French MBT, the EPC (Engin Principal de Combat) will also have a 120mm smoothbore. Only the British are staying with the rifled gun, with the Challenger 120mm, but are developing fin stabilized ammunition for it in order to get the best of both worlds.

Tank ammunition is of two main types, kinetic and chemical energy (KE, CE). The former relies on its speed combined with mass to penetrate armor, and is known as armor piercing ammunition. Being high velocity rounds, they are more accurate than CE types, and are the most favored for killing other tanks. The type used by the tanks of both sides is the armor piercing discarding sabot fin stabilized (APDSFS) round. This consists of a rodlike penetrater made of very dense material like tungsten carbide, with fins on the rear like those on a dart. It is enclosed in a sabot or pot, which brings it up to the caliber of the gun. As the projectile leaves the barrel, the pot separates and flies off, and the energy imparted to the projectile is transferred to the penetrater, which enables it to maintain its velocity and pierce the armor of the opposing tank.

Chemical energy rounds exist in two main forms. High Explosive Plastic (HEP) or, as it is known in Europe, High Explosive Squashhead (HESH), and High Explosive Antitank (HEAT). The HESH or HEP projectile is filled with explosive, and has a soft nose and base fuse. When it strikes the target, the nose flattens and the explosive forms a 'cowpat'. The base fuse is then triggered, detonating the explosive. The resultant shock waves then pass through the armor causing a scab and particles to break off inside, and these will fly at very high velocity. As a means of causing maximum damage inside the tank, HEP is the ideal round. It is also dual purpose as it can be used as a conventional high explosive (HE) round. HEAT, on the other hand, works on an entirely different principle. This is the shaped charge or Monroe effect, named for the US engineer who first discovered it. It consist of an inverted cone with metal liner, behind which is explosive. It has a flat topped casing with a rod on top. This is important, and is there to provide the correct stand off distance without which the round would not work. When the tip of the rod hits the armor, the explosive is detonated and a thin stream of gaseous molten metal, which has very good penetrative powers, passes through the armor penetrating everything in its path. Both these rounds are now available in fin-stabilized form, with the fins opening out once the projectile has left the muzzle.

One other general type of armor defeating ammunition exists, and this combines KE with CE. These rounds are commonly known as Armor Piercing High Explosive (APHE) or Armor Piercing Special Effects (APSE). Here the round penetrates the armor, and then explodes. It is, however, only used on light armored vehicles with smaller caliber guns, and is only effective against thinner skinned targets than MBTs. It is an ideal means of knocking out APCs.

However good the tank gun and its ammunition, they cannot be effective on their own without a good fire control system. Most tank fire control systems now incorporate computers and range finders, which usually make use of lasers. Both tank commander and gunner have their own sights, and the sequence of drill is for the commander to acquire the target, which he indicates to the gunner by automatically lining his sight up with it. The gunner then lays onto the target and takes the range by firing his laser at it. This, and the type of ammunition to be fired are fed into the computer, which automatically puts the gun in the correct ballistic lay. The gunner is now ready to engage. This type of fire control system results in very fast acquisition times, with a high chance of a first round hit. It also means, together, with the recent ammunition developments, that MBTs can now engage their opposite numbers out to ranges of 3000m. Yet, a word of warning must be inserted here.

During World War II tank engagements in NW Europe seldom took place at ranges of greater than 1000m. The postwar tank battles in the Middle East have also generally been fought at this type of range, in spite of increasing firepower improvements. Furthermore surveys of intervisibility in the Central Region have found that it is only possible to see more than 2000m 10% of the time, and the weather also produces a significantly high proportion of days when visibility is low, especially during the winter months. Add to this battlefield obscuration in terms of smoke and dirt thrown up by explosions, and it comes apparent that World War III tank engagements in the Central Region are unlikely to be at long range.

Armored protection traditionally consists of three types. Against KE attack solid armor, usually steel based, which relies on thickness and slope, has always been the most effective. However, this is not so against CE attack. Here spaced or laminated armor are used. The former consists of two separate thicknesses, with a space in between, and the best example is the bazooka or skirting plate which is bolted on to

COMPARISON
T-72
T-64
SOVIET MEDIUM TANKS

NEW 12.7mm MACHINEGUN FIRED FROM OPEN HATCH

DIE-CAST IDLER WHEEL

T-72

IR LIGHT TO RIGHT OF MAIN GUN

SIX LARGE, DIE-CAST ROAD WHEELS

T-72

VENTS ON REAR DECK

T-62 TYPE SNORKEL CARRIED ON LEFT REAR OF TURRET

T-72

The T-64 and T-72 medium tanks are the latest additions to the Soviet armored forces. They feature increased mobility, firepower and improved armor protection over the T-62 medium tank and are a formidable foe for any free-world tank!

TURRET TURNED TO TRAVEL POSITION

T-64 SIX SMALL, STAMPED ROAD WHEELS

12.7mm MACHINEGUN CAN BE FIRED FROM INSIDE TURRET

EXHAUST VENTS AT REAR

T-64

NEW SNORKEL CARRIED ON BACK OF TURRET

IR LIGHT TO LEFT OF MAIN GUN

T-64

T-72 Soviet Medium Tank
Main Armament: 125mm Smoothbore Gun

T-64 Soviet Medium Tank
Main Armament: 125mm Smoothbore Gun

DIA

PREPARED BY THE U.S. ARMY INTELLIGENCE AND THREAT ANALYSIS CENTER (IMAGERY INTELLIGENCE PRODUCTION DIVISION)

1027-79 UNCLASSIFIED

Above: The visual differences between T-64 and T-72. T-72 is being widely exported abroad, unlike T-64, which has not been seen outside the Soviet Army.
Left: T-72 in heavy going.

the side of the tank. Laminated armor consists of layers of different material bonded together. In the last few years a type of this, using new forms of material, has been introduced. Known originally as Chobham armor, after the research establishment in Britain which originally developed it, it has been found to double the protection against HEAT attack, and all the new MBTs in service have adopted it in various forms.

Another means of giving the tank protection is through local smoke, which is produced by firing smoke grenades from launchers situated in banks on the turret. Those on Western tanks are normally designed to give cover over a 140° frontal arc, but it is noticeable that those on the later marks of the T-72 give a much narrower arc. The inference is that the smoke is laid down to advance through, rather than withdraw behind.

81

All MBTs now use diesel engines, since this fuel is less inflammable than petrol and gives better fuel consumption. Apart from the British, whose tanks have tended to have relative low top speeds, the MBTs of both sides are capable of travelling up to 45mph. One limitation on speed is the ability of the crew to stand up to high speeds when traveling cross-country. Unless suspension systems are sufficiently robust, there is the danger that the crew will be too shaken up to fight efficiently.

During World War II tanks, lacking night vision devices, apart from searchlights, were limited during the hours of darkness. Since then, with the develop-

ment of infrared and image intensification, which works on the principle of concentrating the ambient light, the MBT can fight almost as well by night as by day. This does, however, put a much greater strain on the crew. Traditionally this consists of four men – commander, gunner, loader/radio operator and driver. While current Western MBTs have retained this configuration, the Soviet T-64 and T-72 have only a three-man crew. The loader/operator has been removed and an autoloader installed. The advantages of this are that space can be saved, giving an overall smaller vehicle, and loading of the gun is quicker. Conversely, the autoloader must be mechanically

Left: The Chieftain Main Battle Tank which has been in service for nearly 20 years and is likely to remain so for many more in spite of the introduction of Challenger.
Top: Challenger, which reinforces the British belief in the rifled gun.
Above: Striker, which mounts the Swingfire ATGW and is used by the British and Belgians. It has a range of 4000m.

reliable if it is to be of value. Also, the strains of the 24 hour battlefield day on a three-man crew are more severe than for four men.

Soviet armies are either tank or infantry heavy, and vary in size and makeup. Thus the five armies of GSFG are each organized differently. While 20th Guards Army has three motor rifle divisions only, and 8th Guards Army has the same, but with the addition of one tank division, 2nd Guards Army is a balanced formation with two of each. The two tank heavy armies, 3rd Shock Army and 1st Guards Tank Army have three tank and one motor rifle, and four tank and one rifle divisions respectively. In essence, motor

rifle formations are used for the break in operation, while the tank formations exploit it. OMGs will also be tank heavy. However, it must be stressed that the Soviets are believers in combined arms, and the tank division does contain some infantry. The basic organization is three tank and one motor rifle regiment. The former has 94 tanks, divided into three battalions each of three ten tank companies, with one motor rifle company in BMPs as the regiment's infantry element. The infantry regiment, on the other hand, has three motor rifle battalions, also equipped with BMP, and a large tank battalion of 40 tanks, broken down into three companies each of 13 tanks. The lowest tank sub-unit is the three tank platoon, and there are three of these in each tank regiment company, and four in the motor rifle regiment tank companies.

Warsaw Pact tanks normally attack in line abreast, either on their own if the opposition is considered weak, or leading motor rifle elements. The infantry may or may not dismount from their APCs, again dependent on the strength of the defenses. Supporting fire will be supplied by artillery and mortars, with the tanks also firing on the move. Ideally, the Soviets like to fight an encounter battle, catching the enemy on the move, and deploying immediately off the line of march to attack him in the flank. Against prepared defenses, however, a more deliberate attack will be mounted. For the tanks in the tank division the main task is to keep the battle moving and penetrate as fast and as deeply into the enemy's defenses as possible. The infantry with them are there to help deal with small pockets of resistance which cannot be easily bypassed.

The US armored division, of which there are two in the Central Region, 3rd Armored with V(US) Corps and 1st Armored with VII(US) Corps, is much more balanced than its Soviet equivalent and has a more flexible organization. In essence, it has six armor and five mechanized infantry battalions, and three brigade headquarters. The latter equate to the combat commands of World War II and like them do not have a standard mix of infantry and armor under command, but are tailored to suit the situation at the time. In the Division 86 organization the armor battalion is almost twice the size of its Soviet counterpart and has 58 Abrams or M60A3 tanks. These are broken down into four companies each of 14 tanks. These are further split into three platoons of four tanks each. In addition, it has a scout platoon, and a mortar platoon with six 107mm mortars mounted on the M113 APC.

The other NATO armies use the brigade as a fixed formation. The Germans, like the Americans, are in the process of a reorganization, and are slimming down their armor and mechanized infantry battalions to the same size of those of the Soviets, but are providing more of them to each brigade. Thus the new panzer brigade will have three armor battalions, each of 33 Leopard 2s, and one mechanized infantry (panzer grenadier) battalion, as opposed to the former two and one. The Panzer division has two panzer and one panzer grenadier brigades. The British armored division, of which there are three based in Germany, is also organized on a three brigade basis. The majority are 'square' brigades with two armored regiments (equivalent to the US battalion) and two mechanized infantry battalions. Some brigades are, however, armor heavy, with three armored regiments and one mechanized infantry battalion, while others have three mechanized infantry and one

armored unit. The armored regiment is larger than any other NATO tank battalion, with 66 tanks, Chieftain or Challenger, on peacetime establishment, which is increased to 74 in wartime. It has four squadrons, each of four tank troops, a reconnaissance troop and an ATGW troop with Swingfire ATGW mounted on Striker, another member of the CVR(T) family. The Belgian and Dutch armored brigades are also square and use Leopard 1s, although the Dutch are now receiving the Leopard 2.

Like the Warsaw Pact, NATO doctrine stresses the concept of combined arms operations and, in terms of the anti-armor battle, the tank is viewed as but one weapon in the armory, which will combine with the others in order to destroy the enemy tanks and APCs. It is only by inflicting unacceptable losses on these will the Warsaw Pact offensive be halted. In the Sixties and early Seventies, NATO armies were forced to put the majority of their tanks in the front line in order to offset Warsaw superiority in armor. Now, with the rapid increase of other forms of anti-tank weapon available, the need is not so pressing, and NATO is able to keep more armor in reserve for counterattack and counterpenetration, which adds to the depth of the defenses.

Nevertheless, a significant proportion will be involved in the main defensive position, especially in giving anti-armor support to the infantry. Normally tanks remain in hides close to their battle positions, to which they will only deploy when an enemy attack is imminent. Fire positions are taken up ideally on reverse slopes, and one advantage that Western tanks have over their Warsaw Pact counterparts is their ability to depress their guns at a greater angle, which means that the tank presents less of a target. Once a tank does fire, it is very likely to be spotted and, in order to prevent the enemy from engaging it, it will have a number of alternative positions, and will 'jockey' between them after each engagement. As a normal principle, in order to provide the most effective antiarmor defense, the tanks will concentrate on the opposing tanks, while the infantry anti-armor weapons will be used against APCs.

When supporting infantry in the attack, NATO tanks, unlike those of the Warsaw Pact, tend to operate from a flank, shooting the infantry in, and aiming to arrive on the objective at the same time. They also make much more use of fire and movement, with some tanks moving, while others support them from static positions. The Soviets, on the other hand, lay much more emphasis on shock action with firing on the move. All MBTs are now fitted with gun stabilizers to enable them to fire the main and secondary armament with reasonable accuracy on the move, but the chances of a hit are never as good as from a static position, although it can be very effective as suppressive fire to keep the enemy's heads down.

The NATO armor held back in depth is a vitally

important component of the overall defense scheme, especially in the context of the OMG. Its flexibility in its radio communications and ability to deploy quickly from one location to another, make it a very effective counter to the OMG. It can either take up blocking positions in the path of the OMG, which is counterpenetration, or attack it from a flank. Likewise, it will use the same tactics if a major breakthrough takes place. One problem of movement, however, is that by day it is vulnerable to attack by aircraft and attack helicopters, and, wherever possible, all major movement will take place during the hours of darkness.

In the past NATO has always believed that the technical superiority of its tanks would considerably offset numerical inferiority. It is now clear, however, that Soviet tank design, especially with the T-72, has made significant strides forward, especially in terms of firepower and protection. However, a tank is only

as good as its crew, and NATO tankers still have the edge on their Soviet counterparts. Although the latter are being allowed more initiative than hitherto, there is still a rigidity in tactics and training. Nevertheless, the Warsaw Pact armor threat is formidable, and can only be defeated if NATO armor is able to think and act more quickly.

As for the tank itself, some believe that the threats against it have grown so much that its days on the battlefield are numbered. It is accepted that it will not be so prominent on the battlefield, at least on the NATO side, as in the past, but when it is employed, provided that it is at the right place and at the right time, its effect can still be devastating.

Below: An Italian Leopard 1 fords a river. While Soviet tanks have snorkeling equipment, which enables them to cross deep rivers unaided, NATO nations consider that the cost of the equipment is not commensurate with the special training required and risks involved.

Canadian infantry well equipped to face the tough wintry conditions of the Northern Flank of NATO.

The task of infantry in war is to seize and hold ground, and all other arms and services exist to support the infantryman in this. The past 30 years have seen the firepower available to the infantry battalion grow at an impressive rate, both in range and concentration.

In terms of personal weapons, there is a very significant change taking place in both NATO and the Warsaw Pact armies. This is a change of the basic small arms weapon caliber from 7.62mm to 5.56mm and 5.45mm respectively. The main reason for this is that since 1945 there has been a move away from the requirement to be able to engage accurately the enemy at long ranges, towards the need to put down concentrated fire. Both the Warsaw Pact Kalashnikov AK-47 and Belgian FN rifle, which is currently used by a number of NATO armies, recognized this. Although they fired a 7.62mm round, the change from the manual bolt action rifle to semi-automatic weapon, gave a significantly higher rate of fire, but with a maximum effective range of not more than 600m. It was, however, the success of the US Armalite rifle in Vietnam which has perhaps influenced the reduction in caliber more than anything else. Although it fires a 5.56mm round, its lightness compared to 7.62mm weapons, the fact that more ammunition can be carried, and that it compares very favorably to the

Above: US M60 light machine gunner on exercise with blank ammunition.
Top right: Romanian AKM version of AK-47, recognizable by foregrip.
Right: AKM with collapsible butt, which is often used by paratroops.
Bottom right: Soviet RPK-74 5.45mm light machine gun with folding bipod.

Below: Dutch light machine gun team with Belgian FN 7.62mm MAG.

7.62mm in terms of penetration, have led to the adoption of smaller caliber weapon. The Soviets began to replace their AK-47 with the AK-74 in the early Seventies. On the surface it looks very similar, but has a much higher rate of fire, and the 30-round magazine has been replaced by a 90-round magazine.

The US Army has now been equipped with the Armalite, also known as the M16, for some years, although a few of the older M14 7.62mm rifles are still to be found among reserve units. At present a product improvement program on the M16 is taking place, and the M16 A2 will be very much more robust. Its most noticeable feature will be a three round burst capability in place of the fully automatic capability on the M16A1. This should certainly help to conserve ammunition. Looking further into the future,

development work is being undertaken on the Advanced Combat Rifle (ACR), and it is likely to include caseless ammunition and the concept of the multiple bullet as a means of controlling dispersion and thereby obtaining increased accuracy with burst fire. The British, on the other hand, are about to introduce a new system to replace their present FN family. SA80 consists of two weapons, both using the new 5.56mm standard NATO round. The first is known as the Individual Weapon (IW) and will replace both the 9mm submachine gun (SMG) and the selfloading rifle (SLR). The Light Support Weapon (LSW), on the other hand, will replace the General Purpose Machine Gun (GPMG) and the older Light Machine Gun (LMG), the Bren gun of World War II vintage. Other NATO member

Above: Canadian Special Service Force troops fire the 0.30in Browning.
Below: US M16A1 Armalite being fired in wintry conditions.
Below right: The British Army's new 5.56mm Individual Weapon.

Above right: Covered by two RPG-7s Soviet motor riflemen assault with AK-47 light machine gun and assault rifles.
Right: US airborne troops with Armalites and 105mm towed artillery.

nations are also developing similar concepts. Indeed, as its squad automatic weapon, the US Army has adopted the Belgian FN Minimi LMG and has designated it the Squad Automatic Weapon (SAW), and this will replace the M60 7.62mm machine gun. The Soviets, too, have a variant of the AK-74, known as the AKS-74, with folding bipod, which can be used as an LMG and also have the RPK-74, a variant of the PK machine gun, but rebarreled to take 5.45mm ammunition. Thus, the infantry squad of the future will have much heavier firepower and will be able to sustain itself in combat for much longer without resupply than it can do at present.

Like the tanker, the infantryman is also obtaining better and better night fighting aids, and individual weapon night sights, using image intensification, are becoming very effective. At squad level, too, the grenade plays an important part, especially the US M79 grenade launcher, which is in service with a number of NATO armies and fires a 40mm grenade. Grenades are either HE, antitank or smoke.

As far as support weapons are concerned, the mortar is particularly important. The Warsaw Pact has a wide range of calibers. They have recently replaced the 82mm mortar in the mortar platoon of the motor rifle battalion with the 120mm, which fires a bomb with over four times the weight of that of its predecessor out to a range of almost 6km, with a rate of fire of 15 bombs per minute. The Soviets also have 160mm and 240mm mortars, but these are an artillery

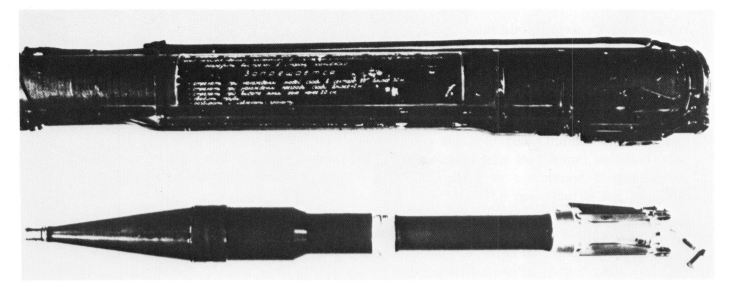

Above: The RPG-16 which is replacing the RPG-7 in Soviet service.
Left: On maneuvers, a tank hunting team surprises M60 tanks.
Below: Milan is now the most common type of NATO medium range ATGW.

responsibility. The standard NATO mortar is the 81mm with a range of almost 6km, but the 107mm (4.5in) is also used. The key to the mortar is that it is the infantry battalion's own integral artillery, and that it can bring down an impressive concentration of fire very quickly. Furthermore, being a high trajectory weapon, it is particularly effective against dug-in infantry.

What concerns the infantry most is its ability to deal with the armor threat, and the modern infantry battalion has a wide range of weapons to do this. Antitank grenades have already been mentioned, but these are only effective at ranges of 20–30m and against thinner armor. Thus they are not suitable against an MBT. The next category is the handheld weapon, which fires a HEAT warhead. Perhaps the most well known of these is the Soviet RPG-7, which is very popular among insurgent forces throughout the world. This fires an 85mm projectile, but is being replaced by the RPG-16 with a 73mm warhead. The Czechs also have the RPG P-27 with a 45mm war-

head. On the NATO side, this type of weapon comes in the form of the light antitank weapon (LAW) and medium antitank weapon (MAW), which are found at squad and platoon level respectively. The LAW is a 66mm disposable launcher found at squad level, and is ideal for tank hunting parties, or for combating armor in close country. MAW is a platoon weapon, and in many European NATO armies this is the 84mm Carl Gustav, which also fires a HEAT warhead with an effective range of 400m. The Germans, however, have replaced this with ATGW, while the US Army, which previously had the 90mm recoilless rifle, have done the same.

In terms of antitank weapons it is ATGW which has been the 'growth industry' on the battlefield during the past twenty years. No better demonstration of their effectiveness has occurred than during the opening days of the 1973 Yom Kippur War, when Soviet made Saggers in Egyptian hands put paid to the omnipotence of the Israeli tank on the battlefield. Indeed, it was this and heliborne ATGW, which

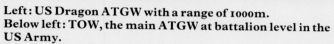
Left: US Dragon ATGW with a range of 1000m.
Below left: TOW, the main ATGW at battalion level in the US Army.
Above: The 2nd Generation Soviet AT-4 Spigot ATGW.
Right: AT-3 Sagger, which was so successful in the 1973 Yom Kippur War.
Below: Canadians firing the obsolescent 106mm recoilless rifle.

caused some 'instant experts' to state that ATGW had sounded the death knell for the tank. They have made the tank more wary, but have not eradicated it. Nevertheless, they are a significant threat. What its introduction has done in particular for the infantryman is to give him an armor defeating capability at twice the range of the recoilless guns which he had before.

All ATGW systems have HEAT warheads. The missile is guided onto the target using what is known as command guidance, which means that the operator has to give the missile commands. First generation ATGW normally had manual command to line of sight, which meant that the controller had to first gather the missile, and then manuever it onto the line between his eye and the target and maintain it on this line. The main problem, as the French first found in Algeria, is that the controller under the stress of battle finds this difficult to do. Consequently the second generation missiles are on semiautomatic command to line of sight (SACLOS). Here the controller merely has to keep his sight on the target and a computer gives the missile signals to enable it to fly along the line of sight. The US Army's TOW missile is a very good example of this, and has a range which has been increased over the years from 2000 to 3750m and is the infantry battalion's primary anti-armor weapon. It also has a thermal-imaging infrared night sight, which enables it to be used in darkness and poor visibility. The European NATO nations use the Franco-German Milan system. In terms of MAW, the US also has Dragon, with a range out to 1000m. As a heavy ATGW system, the British and Belgians use Swingfire, but this is found with armored units and on helicopters, rather than in infantry battalions.

One minor problem with ATGW systems is that because the missile has to be gathered, there is a minimum effective range, which is usually about 200m. However, it is the relatively long maximum effective range which needs to be exploited, and hence ATGW is always sited where it has a good field of fire, and can pick off enemy armor at long range. Vehicle mounted systems can also be fired in the separated mode, which means that the controller can be separated as much as 300m from the launcher vehicle, but is positioned down behind cover.

The Soviet ATGW systems are numerous. Snapper, Swatter and Sagger belong to the first generation, but the Swatter-B and Sagger-B now have SACLOS incorporated. Spigot and Spandrel have also been introduced as second generation systems. Their ranges tend to be lower than their NATO counterparts, with none above 3000m. Again, they are either manportable or carried in vehicles. Indeed, almost every type of light armored vehicle is equipped with some form of ATGW. Unlike NATO, the Soviets still believe in the traditional towed anti-

Left: Another view of TOW, this time in Italian hands.
Above: The US Improved TOW (TOW 2) showing initial flight stages.
Below: A Canadian M-72 66mm disposable LAW.

tank gun, and the latest model the 100mm T-12 has a smoothbore gun and fires APDSFS ammunition, which will penetrate 400mm of armored plate at 500m range. A battalion of these is found in every motor rifle division.

Currently, however, there is concern, in the light of improvements to tank armor, over the effectiveness of current infantry manned anti-armor weapons, especially ATGW. HEAT warhead effectiveness is very much dependent on diameter, and it is noteworthy that the US Army is now introducing TOW 2 into service with the diameter of the warhead increased from four to six inches in order to successfully engage T-64 and T-72 frontal armor. It is likely that other countries will follow this example.

The past two decades have been the era of the mechanized infantryman with his ability to move quickly about the battlefield. Initially, his vehicle was the APC, which in NATO eyes was little more than a battlefield cab, usually armed with no more than a 7.62mm machine gun. The idea was that it carried the infantry to their deployment position, dropped them off and then retired to the rear, collecting them again when they had finished their task. Even in the attack, the normal practice was for the infantry to debuss short of their objective and make the final assault on foot. The Soviets, however, have always attached much importance to the infantry remaining mounted as much as possible in order to

97

maintain the momentum of the assault, and it was this that caused them to introduce a new type of infantry AFV.

When the BMP-1 first made its appearance in the late Sixties it caused a considerable stir in NATO. Armed with a 73mm smoothbore gun and Sagger ATGW launcher, it was a true armored fighting vehicle rather than merely a transport vehicle, which the infantry could actually fight from. The need to dismount would in the future be much less. The West Germans, however, were not far behind. Drawing on their World War II panzer grenadier experience, they brought Marder into service in 1972, which is armed with a 20mm cannon and 7.62 mm machine gun. Other Western nations were somewhat slower in producing Mechanized Infantry Combat Vehicles (MICV), as they are called. The British experimented with a Rarden 30mm gun mounted on top of their FV432 APC, but discarded the idea, and are now about to bring MCV-80 into service, which will also have a 30mm Rarden on the basic version. US efforts in this field have resulted in the M2 Bradley, with 25mm cannon and TOW missile launchers. At present, however, many NATO nations are still reliant on the APC, the ubiquitous M113, although the Dutch and Belgians have the US private venture FMC Armored Infantry Fighting Vehicle (AIFV).

Above: The ubiquitous M113 APC with US infantry dismounting.
Right: The French AMX VTP M56 MICV, which is now being replaced by the AMX-10P.
Below right: The German Marder with 20mm cannon.

Although the Soviets see the MICV as helping considerably in maintaining the momentum of the attack, within NATO there is still much discussion as to how it should be used in defense. On the surface it is seen as a valuable addition to the antiarmor battle, with the firepower available to knock out like vehicles, which means that tanks and ATGW can concentrate on knocking out the opposing tanks. There are two snags to this. Firstly, it is still the mechanized infantry's means of transport and, if introduced into the firing line, there is the danger of it being knocked out, which will deprive the infantry of their mobility. Then again, if the infantry are dismounted and dug in, to have MICVs operating too close to them is likely to bring down enemy artillery fire onto their positions. It is therefore very likely that a proportion will be held back out of the immediate battle in order to safeguard the mobility of the infantry, while the remainder will operate with the tanks, away from the infantry positions.

The Soviet Motor Rifle division consists of three motor rifle and one tank regiment. The tank regiment

Left: Backbone of the Soviet Motor Rifle Division is the BTR-60PB. Latest version, BTR-70 has a lengthened hull and larger engine compartment.
Below left: US M113 APC in Germany.
Right: US airborne troops being used in the light infantry role.

has the same organization as in the tank division, while the motor rifle regiment has a tank battalion of 40 tanks, and three motor rifle battalions, each of three companies of three platoons each. The platoon has three MICVs or APCs, with a further one at company headquarters. One of the regiments is equipped with BMP, as in the tank division, while the others have the BTR-60PB APC, which mounts 14.5mm and 7.62mm machine guns. Also found in the regiment is an ATGW company with nine BRDM-2s mounting Spandrel. Recently, the tank strength of the motor rifle division has been increased by adding an independent tank battalion of 50 tanks to it. It also has a reconnaissance battalion, as mentioned in Chapter 4, and an antitank battalion with 18 T-12 100mm smoothbore antitank guns. In total, it has a strength of some 12,000 men with 265 tanks and over 400 MICVs/APCs.

The US Division 86 mechanized infantry division is organized very much like its armored counterpart, with three brigade headquarters under which battalions will be placed under command, dependent on the tactical situation. Currently, each of the US corps in Germany has one complete mechanized division on the ground, 8 Mech Inf Div with V(US) Corps and 3 Mech Inf Div with VII(US) Corps. Each also has a brigade of 4 and 1 Mech Divs respectively, with the balance to be deployed from CONUS when hostilities are imminent. The mechanized division has four armor battalions and six mechanized infantry battalions. The latter are very much based on the Bradley IFV, and each has four rifle companies. These are broken down into three platoons, each of three M2 Bradleys, with a further two at company headquarters. In addition, the mechanized battalion has a scout platoon with six M3 Bradley CFVs, an antitank company with twelve TOW 2s and a mortar platoon with six 107mm mortars mounted in M113s.

The German panzer grenadier division has two armored infantry brigades and one tank brigade. The former now has two tank battalions and two armored infantry battalions, each with 33 MICVs. In addition, it has a light infantry battalion mounted in light trucks or M113s, which is kept only at cadre strength in peacetime. The British mechanized battalion is organized on very similar lines to the American, with four rifle companies each of three platoons, and also had a support company with an 81mm mortar platoon and an antitank platoon with 16 Milan launcher systems. Both the Belgians and the Dutch have slimmer mechanized infantry brigades, with only two mechanized and one tank battalions. They also have TOW ATGW companies at brigade level.

There is no doubt that if there was a conflict in the Central Region, it would be the mechanized infantry of both sides who would bear the initial brunt of the fighting. While the Warsaw Pact infantry would

Above: M113s followed by an M60 pass through a German village.
Below: A Soviet BMP MICV with 73mm smoothbore gun. The BMP-80 has a two man turret with 30mm gun.
Above right: Soviet Naval Infantry with a BTR-60P.
Right: The US Marine Corps' amphibious LVT7A1.

Left: An M113 TOW mounting.
Below left: A hasty meal during Ex Reforger 82.

Top: Canadian infantry on Northern Flank.
Bottom: French infantry supported by VAB APCs and, in background, AMX-13 light tanks.

attempt to remain mounted as long as possible, the bulk of NATO mechanized infantry will be dismounted and dug in, with at least some of their MICVs joining in the armor battle. They will try and destroy the Warsaw Pact infantry while they are still inside their vehicles, and those that do dismount will be engaged with small arms fire. There, are, however, other types of infantry who will also play their part in the battle.

One very noticeable change to the geography of the Central Region during the past thirty years has been the rapid growth of built up areas, what is known as conurbization. This clearly favors the defender, and both sides have recently begun to pay serious attention to Fighting in Built Up Areas (FIBUA). The Soviets realize that they cannot avoid them, and that they will slow down the momentum of the advance. The specter of the fighting in the streets of Stalingrad, Budapest and Berlin during the Great Patriotic War is there to haunt. Of particular concern is the ability of the defender to throw up effective defenses in villages and use antitank weapons from them in large quantities. In the past, FIBUA was a slow business, especially in towns, and meant a gradual crumbling of the enemy's defenses. Now, when attacking towns, the Soviets are planning to mount raids designed to secure key objectives in the center as a means of maintaining momentum. As for lower level defenses in villages, there is a realization that these can only be quickly overcome if the soldier on the ground is encouraged to use his initiative, but for the enlisted man, noncom or junior officer, this, of course, runs rather contrary to his training for general battle.

NATO, on the other hand, is appreciating more and more that integrating existing built-up areas into the defense plan will make it that much more effective. The defense of villages is an ideal task for light infantry, and it has already been noted that each German panzergrenadier brigade has a light infantry battalion. The US Army, too, has set up an experimental light division, although this is not with the Central Region specifically in mind. The British also make use of light infantry, mainly territorial battalions which will reinforce 1(BR) Corps in war. Indeed, 2nd Infantry Division consists very largely of light infantry, although its task is more than just the defense of villages. The German *Teritorialheer* also consists of a large number of light infantry units, one of whose major roles is the defense of urban areas. As yet, however, no effort has been made to prepare village defenses in time of peace since there could be political problems involved. Nevertheless, if the Federal Republic were to agree to a modicum of preparation in peacetime, the NATO defenses would be even more enhanced.

The other primary role of light infantry at present is that of rear area security. In the Central Region,

Top left: Soviet LPO-50 flamethrower – particularly useful for fighting in built up areas.
Left: Soviet 82mm M1937 mortar.
Bottom left: An armored CCC vehicle developed for the US Army.
Above: Live firing practice.
Below: US mechanized infantry put in a dismounted attack.

this is mainly the task of the German *Territorialheer*, or Territorial Command. In particular it has responsibility for the defense of the territory behind the frontline NATO corps, and is divided into two subcommands for this purpose, German Territorial Northern Command (GTNC) which supports NORTHAG and German Territorial Southern Command (GTSC) with CENTAG. Their main tasks are the guarding of vital supply routes, key bridges across waterways and vulnerable points like power stations, ammunition depots and communication centers. In the rear part of the national corps areas of operations, light infantry are also employed on much the same tasks, but also as quick reaction forces in the event of airborne or heliborne landings. This brings in the use of light infantry in the heliborne role, and is covered in Chapter 8.

One other type of infantry which is also used in the Central Region is mountain infantry. The most southern of the NATO divisions, which comes under II(GE) Corps, is the German 1st Mountain Division. This is made up of one armored, one mechanized infantry and one mountain brigade, with the last named having four mountain infantry battalions. They are trained in mountain climbing and skiing and, although they have wheeled transport, they also use mules to a large extent. Mountain infantry is also employed by the Italians, in the form of the famous Alpini, and on the flanks of NATO. The Soviets, too, have three mountain divisions.

In spite of the ever increasing technology of the land battle, infantry still have a vital role to play, not just in ever more sophisticated AFVs, but also on their feet or dug in. Apart from seizing and holding ground, they also act as a shoulder or anchor for the mobile forces fighting around them. The infantryman remains concerned by the armor threat, although he is better equipped to combat it than ever before. What tends to worry him more is the ever increasing power of artillery.

6. ARTILLERY

'God fights on the side with the best artillery' Napoleon Bonaparte was reputed to have said, and indeed it has played a very dominant part on the 20th Century battlefield. Time and again it has been the quick and effective response of artillery which has turned the fortunes of both defender and attacker. Moreover, any soldier on the battlefield of today feels that much more confident in the knowledge that his own artillery is available to support him at a moment's notice.

Artillery is generally divided into three main types – nuclear, which was covered in Chapter 3, conventional and air defense. Conventional artillery has a number of tactical roles, all tied in to the support of armor and infantry. Close support artillery is designed to give intimate support to combat units, while general support artillery gives a heavier weight of fire, which is used to reinforce close support artillery, to counter enemy artillery, long range harrassing of the enemy, and interdiction tasks. Locating artillery pinpoints enemy guns, mortars and missile systems so that they can be engaged by retaliatory fire, as well as providing a surveillance capability through the use of drones and Remotely Piloted Vehicles (RPV), and meteorological and survey data, which is essential for the guns to lay down accurate fire.

Both the Warsaw Pact and NATO recognize similar types of fire. In defense the most vital type is what is known as Defensive Fire (DF). This is fire put down on pre-agreed targets – enemy forming up places, likely approaches etc. Most crucial is, in NATO parlance, the Final Preventive Fire (FPF) target, which is usually linear and placed just in front of the defenses and is used when the enemy is poised to overrun them. In the attack the main two types are preparation fire, which is used to soften the defenses up before the attack, and covering fire, which, as it implies, keeps the enemy's heads down while the attack is going in. The Soviets subdivide covering fire into close support fire, which is that delivered during the assault, and accompaniment fire, which is fired from guns accompanying the attacking troops in to the depths of an extensive defensive position. If the attacker pauses to reorganize on the objective, he may well have to use DF in the event of an enemy counterattack. Other types of fire, which might be used in both defense and attack, are harrassing fire, which is designed to interfere with enemy movement and lower morale, counter battery (CB) fire against enemy artillery, smoke, illuminating and marking.

Fire can either be observed or predicted. The former is the more accurate, in that the guns can be visually corrected onto the target, and this is usually done by forward observers (FO), who will be with the forward tank and infantry subunits. However, certainly in NATO armies, every platoon leader and tank commander is trained to correct artillery fire,

Previous pages: British Army M109 155mm selfpropelled howitzer.
Above: The US M101 105mm towed howitzer, with excellent elevation.
Above right: US M109 155mm SP howitzer, here manned by the Bundeswehr, is used by most NATO armies.
Right: Canadian L-5 105mm towed howitzer is, like the US M101, unlikely to be used in the Central Region, but more on the flanks of NATO.

and may well have to do it when the FO cannot see or identify the target. Predicted fire to be effective requires accurate survey and current meteorological information, as well as accurate map coordinates of the target. Computers now make this possible, and can give instant readouts on the laying details for each gun. Those like the US Field Artillery Digital Computer (FADAC) can also store the details of up to 30 targets, and this is especially useful for DFs.

Left: FH70 155mm wheeled howitzer, which was developed jointly by the British, Germans and Italians.
Below: Lance, which carries both conventional and nuclear warheads to a range of 25 miles.

If artillery fire is to be instantaneously responsive, communications between the FO, the fire control center and the guns must be efficient. To this end, the US Army has introduced the Tacfire system at artillery battalion level and above. Using a digital message entry device, the FO can pass fire directions directly into a computer, where they are quickly checked by the fire direction officer, and passed to the guns in just a few seconds. At battery level, FADAC has now been replaced by the Battery Computer System (BCS), which is compatible with Tacfire, and this operates very much on the same principle.

The most common NATO gun is the US M109 155mm self-propelled howitzer, which has now been in service with almost all NATO armies for some 20 years. This has a range over 18,000m, which can be boosted to 24,000m with rocket assisted projectiles. The British still have the 105mm self-propelled Abbot in their close support artillery, but this will be replaced shortly by SP70, a 155mm howitzer, which has been developed jointly with the Germans and the Italians. NATO general support artillery is virtually wholly American in origin, and is made up of the M107 175mm, which has been up until now the main counter battery weapon, and the M110 203mm. The A2 version of the latter has now replaced the M110 in the US Army, and fires a rocket assisted round out to 30,000m and a conventional round to just over 24,000m. In the Central Region almost all NATO guns are self-propelled, although the German mountain division does have the FH70 155mm towed gun. This, like SP70, was developed by the British, Germans and Italians jointly. Light infantry, too, have wheeled guns, and here the US M198 155mm howitzer is making an increasing appearance.

While Pershing is a nuclear dedicated weapon, Lance can be used with a conventional warhead as well, and the most popular version contains a large number of bomblets. Lance uses an inertial guidance system, whereby details of the launch and target positions and the desired flight path are fed into a computer carried by the missile, which ensures that the missile maintains the correct flight path.

Another general support system which is just entering the NATO armory is the Multiple-Launch Rocket System (MLRS). This consists of 12 launchers mounted on an M2 Bradley chassis, which will fire 230mm rockets to ranges in excess of 30km, either singly or in a ripple mode, which enables all 12 to be launched in less than a minute. The warhead consists of 644 M77 submunitions, which combine a shaped charge with fragmentation. The complete load of rockets can effectively cover an area of 30,000 square yards, and is particularly effective in the counterbattery role. Developed by the US, the British, French, West Germans and Italians will begin manufacturing them under licence by the end of the Eighties.

Below: Soviet M-1973 152mm SP howitzer.
Right: 122mm D-30 howitzer, which is still found in both Soviet tank and motor rifle divisions.

Up until the early Seventies Warsaw Pact artillery guns were all towed. The Soviets, however, became increasingly concerned over the growing power of the NATO defenses and the need to be able to penetrate them quickly. One way of making this possible was to have artillery much further forward than previously, but towed artillery is obviously very vulnerable. Hence, they introduced the M-1974 122mm self-propelled howitzer, with a range of 15,000m with conventional ammunition and 21,000m with rocket assisted projectiles, and the M-1973 152mm howitzer with a range of 18,500m. Nevertheless, they still have much artillery. Most common is the 122mm D-30 gun/howitzer, which has a high rate of fire of eight rounds per minute. The 130mm M-54 and 152mm M-55 D-20 are also found. In the satellite armies, and Soviet second-line divisions,

the earlier M-38 122mm, M-43 130mm and M-37 152mm are still used. The Soviets have also recently deployed a 203mm self-propelled howitzer which matches the US M110.

The Soviet Frog and Scud series of tactical rocket launchers are, like Lance, capable of firing both conventional and nuclear warheads, as are the medium range Shaddock, Scaleboard and Shyster. Frog-7 has a range of 60km, while that of Scud-B is almost five times the distance. The medium range missiles have ranges of 1000km and beyond, and are unlikely to affect the immediate battle. Unlike NATO, which has only recently woken up to the value of MLRS, the Soviets have always considered it as an essential support fire weapon. The most common system is the BM-21, which has 40 122mm rocket launcher tubes, and can fire the full load off in 30

seconds, although it takes 10–15 minutes to reload.
The BM-24 240mm 12 tube system is also in service,
but both this and BM-21 are likely to be replaced by
the new BM-27, which is also 240mm, but has 16
tubes. 130mm, 140mm, 200mm and 250mm systems
are also found, especially among the satellite armies.
All Warsaw Pact MLRS is truckborne, except for the
140mm 16 tube RPU-14 system which is towed and
used by airborne troops.

The lowest level at which artillery is found in the
Soviet Army is at regimental level. While the tank
regiment does not have its own integral field artillery,
the BMP motor rifle regiment has a battalion of
eighteen M-1974 122mm guns, while its BTR60
counterpart has a battalion of 122mm towed howitzers. At divisional level, both types of division have
two 122mm towed howitzer battalions and one
M-1973 152mm SP howitzer battalion. In all these
battalions there are three six gun batteries. Also at
division is a heavy rocket launcher battalion with four
Frog-4 or 7 and a rocket launcher battalion with
eighteen BM-21, also divided into three batteries. At
army level there is further artillery found in the form
of an artillery brigade and a rocket launcher brigade.
The artillery brigade includes two battalions of M-54
130mm towed howitzers and a battalion of 152mm
guns. In tank armies the latter is the M-1973, while
other armies have the towed M-37. Armies other than
tank also have a battalion of 85mm or 100mm antitank
guns. The rocket launcher brigades have three battalions each of four Scud. Even more additional
artillery is found at front level, with a complete
artillery division of three brigades, organized on the
same lines as the army artillery brigades, as well as a
heavy rocket brigade with Scud and Scaleboard.
Thus, by way of example, GSFG has the 34th
Artillery Division to support its five armies.

The mass of artillery available to the Soviets indicates that their traditional belief in it, especially borne of the massive barrages which they mounted on the Eastern Front during the Great Patriotic War, still holds very firm. In terms of organizing it for a particular operation, the practice is to form artillery groups, which can be at any level from regiment through division to front or army. In order to decide how much artillery is required, the Soviets have laid down artillery norms. For a start, they precisely define three levels of destruction. Neutralization is designed to cause minimum damage, but will temporarily paralyze the defense during and just after the bombardment. Suppression is defined as 25% destruction of men and equipment, while total destruction is 60% or more casualties to men and materiel, with the result that the target no longer has any military value. Against a carefully prepared defense it is calculated that 200 rounds of 122mm will be required per hectare (100 × 100m) to suppress it, but only 150 rounds if it is a hasty defense. This represents 0.7lbs of explosive on every square meter in the latter case, and almost 1lb in the former. British studies of the fighting in NW Europe during 1944–5 concluded that as little as 0.25lbs of explosive per square yard was sufficient to cause a complete breakdown of morale if fired over a short period of time, 15 minutes, and this is similar to the length of the preparatory bombardment envisaged by the Soviets. Indeed, it is not the physical destruction caused by artillery fire, but the effect on morale which causes defenses to cave in. Since NATO forward troops may have little time in which to prepare their defenses, there is much study at present into methods of constructing shellproof positions quickly so that the effects of this type of bombardment are minimized. Nevertheless, these Soviet norms are ambitious, and will need a large number of guns to achieve them. The ammunition expenditure will also be high, which will require a very efficient resupply system.

NATO direct support artillery is generally organized on the basis of one battalion of eighteen guns being in direct support of each brigade. By direct support is meant that the fire of those guns is guaranteed to that brigade at all times. In turn the brigade commander will allocate the three batteries to the direct support of battalion task forces, which are a mix of armor and infantry. In order to build flexibility into the system, batteries can also be placed in support of combat units. This means that when they are not involved in giving supporting fire to the unit in which they are in direct support, they are available to other units. In the US and British corps this close support artillery is controlled at divisional level, but in other armies it is integral to the brigade organization. In the general support role at divisional level the US has one M110 battalion and will also have an MLRS battery of nine launchers. The Germans have a four battery battalion at divisional level, two M107 and two M110. They also have a locating battalion and a rocket battalion, which has one Lance battery and two MLRS batteries. The other NATO armies keep their general support artillery pooled at Corps level, but will place elements of it in support of the divisions. Thus the British have a four battery M107 battalion and a locating battalion, as well as a Lance battalion. While the last will always be retained under corps control, the other two elements will give support to the forward divisions.

NATO artillery commanders do not strive to achieve laid down norms like their Warsaw Pact opposite numbers, and tend to do their fire planning in terms of what is available and how much ammunition they have. They also have laid down rates of fire. Thus for an M109, burst fire can either be three rounds in one minute or six rounds over three minutes. Anything above this is considered sustained fire and will be at a rate of one round per minute. On this basis targets will be engaged for set periods of time and at particular rates of fire. What is stressed very highly in NATO armies is that artillery representatives at all levels must keep physically very close to the commanders whom they are supporting so that they can react quickly as well as be able to give immediate advice on artillery matters.

The main type of artillery ammunition is the HE round. These can either be ground or air burst. Smoke rounds are also used extensively to cover movement, as well as illuminating rounds by night. Target indicating rounds, using colored smoke are employed to guide ground attack aircraft onto targets. Most artillery guns also have an anti-armor round, normally HEP or HESH for NATO and HEAT for the Warsaw Pact, and can be used in the direct fire role if necessary. Indeed, Soviet self-propelled artillery is often used this way when giving accompanying fire during an assault.

The last few years, however, have seen two developments which are about to radically affect the power of artillery. The first of these is the submunition. The US MLRS rocket warhead has already been described, but conventional artillery 155mm and 203mm rounds are also being developed by the US to release dual purpose anti-armor and anti-personnel submunitions. The 203mm round has 180 of these, while the 155mm has 88. This gives artillery much more flexibility and an ability to destroy armor at long range. The fact that the latter is attacked on its top armor, which until now has always been relatively thin as a means of saving weight, is of particular concern to tank designers.

Top: Soviet FROG-7 firing unit and its crew.
Top right: German 110mm LARS MLRS which will be replaced by the US system.
Right: Soviet BM-21 MLRS.

The other new form of munition is the Precision Guided Missile (PGM). In the early 1970s the US produced a new concept, that of Cannon Launched Guided Projectiles (CLGP), which became known as Copperhead. The idea is to use laser to guide an artillery round onto a precision target, and in this case it was the tank which was very much in mind. Using an observer with a laser designater to identify the target, the Copperhead round is fired and when it gets into the target area, sensors in its nose pick up the reflected laser energy and it homes in on the target. For a decade, however, Copperhead has suffered problems in that it has not been able to achieve the laid down accuracy of 90%, and was for a time canceled. Recently, the accuracy has improved, and the US Army has ordered some, but at over $50,000 per round it has become an expensive means of killing a tank. In the meantime, a more effective anti-armor precision round is being developed. Sense-and-Destroy Armor System (SADARMS) works on the principle of having a radar sensor to detect armor. The round, which is to be fired from the M110, as opposed to M109 for Copperhead, contains three antiarmor submunitions, each of which has a radar sensor in it. They are ejected from the carrier shell by time fuse. Suspended by parachute, the

Above: How Copperhead works. Targets are designated by helicopter, aircraft or MICV and then engaged by the guns in the foreground, who need to merely know the map square in which the target is in.
Top right: Soviet SA-7 GRAIL SAM, which is being replaced by STRELA-2.
Far right: British Blowpipe SAM in action in the Falklands.
Right: The highly effective ZSU-23-4.

sensor scans the ground below it and when an AFV is detected it locks on to it, and the submunition lands on top of the vehicle. This concept, and ones like it, are now being developed by the US Army and US Air Force in conjunction for use with medium range missiles and, combined with MLRS, indicates a very feasible method of offsetting Warsaw Pact numerical superiority in armor using conventional means.

The air threat is of very great concern to both sides, and air defense artillery is another vital ingredient of the land forces of both sides. Aircraft in the ground support role can have a decisive influence on the battlefield, especially if they are operating in conditions of air superiority. In particular it is their ability to inhibit movement. As friendly air forces never have enough aircraft to fully carry out all the roles assigned to them, they cannot be expected to keep the enemy's air entirely off the ground troops.

Air defense artillery comes in two types, missile and gun. In order to discuss the use of the two, it is simplest to consider them in terms of the NATO height band definitions which are:

Very Low Level – below 150m
Low Level – 150–600m
Medium Level – 600–7500m
High Level – 7500–15,000m
Very High Level – above 15,000m

At very low level, aircraft and helicopters can be engaged initially by small arms fire. Many AFVs of both sides have air defense 7.62mm machine guns mounted and these, together with cannon, can be used. However, the aircraft, and more especially the helicopter, which will be contour flying, will be only fleeting targets, and it is most unlikely that ground troops will acquire them in time to engage, let alone put up effective fire because of the speed of the target.

The problem is very much the same when dealing with low level aircraft. Here, however, the individual surface-to-air (SAM) missiles can also be used. The Soviet SAM-7 Grail has been used extensively in the Middle East and by the Vietcong and North Vietnamese with varying success. It is a heat seeking weapon using infrared guidance, which makes it a 'fire and forget' system, but also means that it is a tail chaser, which can only engage an aircraft once it has made its attack. Even then it would have to be traveling relatively slowly for the missile to catch it up. Recently the Soviets have introduced an improved version called Strela-2, which has increased velocity and range, which for SAM-7 is 3600m up to a height of 1500m. The US Redeye is very similar, but is now being replaced by the Stinger, with an improved guidance system, still infrared, which enables it to engage targets from all angles. It also has an Identification Friend-or-Foe (IFF) system and, operating in the ultraviolet, as well as infrared, is less vulnerable to countermeasures, the most usual of which is for the target aircraft to drop flares to divert the missile. Its range is also increased to some 5000m, and it can travel at Mach 2. The British Blowpipe is a manual command to line of sight (MACLOS) system, which means that it can engage a target from any angle, being non heat seeking.

The more sophisticated gun systems can be very effective at low level. These incorporate a radar which picks up the enemy aircraft and then passes signals which bring the weapons system automatically on target. Most famous of these is the Soviet ZSU-23-4, which has quadruple 23mm cannon mounted in a turret on a PT-76 light amphibious tank chassis. It can, using all four guns, fire 4000 rounds per minute and take on targets up to 3000m in range. It had much success during the Yom Kippur war against Israeli aircraft which had been forced to fly low because of the missile threat. The German Gepard, with two 35mm rapid fire guns, also has an

Top: US Vulcan system mounted on an M113 variant, M163A1.
Right: Vulcan tactically deployed in order to cover all possible air approaches.
Below right: British Tracked Rapier, now coming into service and likely to be even more responsive than the towed version.

impressive performance, and is used by the Dutch as well. The current US Army system is Vulcan, which works on the Gatling principle, with six revolving 20mm barrels. However, it is limited by weather and daylight, although it has a crude radar system, and is about to be replaced by the Sergeant York. This has twin Swedish Bofors 40mm, a much more effective air defense weapon than the 20mm, and is mounted on an M60 tank chassis. It has a maximum effective horizontal range of 4000m and can engage up to a height of 3000m.

At medium height another range of air defense weapons comes into play. In Warsaw Pact armies this is represented by the SAM-8 Gecko and SAM-9 Gaskin with horizontal maximum ranges of 12km and 7km respectively, and vertical ranges of 6km and 5km. While Gecko is mounted on a 6 × 6 truck, Gaskin uses the BRDM-2. The US equivalent is Chaparral, with a 4800m maximum horizontal range and a height of 2500m, and mounted on the M730 tracked chassis. It was the intention to replace this with the Franco-German Roland system, but this was cancelled for budgetary reasons in 1981, and improvements are now being made to make Chaparral more effective. Roland is popular with a number of Continental European NATO armies and is usually mounted on a Marder chassis. It can engage aircraft flying up to speeds of Mach 1.5 at a horizontal range of over 20km up to a height of almost 1700m. The other major system in this family is the British Rapier, which had much success in the Falklands. This has a horizontal range of 7km and can engage aircraft up to a height of 3000m. Until now it has been mounted on a wheeled trailer, but is being put on tracks to give it added mobility.

Weapons operating in the high and very high level bands are all missiles, and Warsaw Pact examples are the SA-5 Gammon and SA-6 Gainful. On the NATO side, the US is carrying out an improvement program on its Hawk missile, which has been in service since 1960. Improved Hawk has a horizontal range of 40km and can engage aircraft from heights of 30m to 12,000km. Further back is found the Nike-Hercules system, but this is now being replaced by Patriot, which is designed to counter large numbers of high speed aircraft and short range missiles at all altitudes. It was originally planned that Patriot would

Above: The Euromissile Roland SAM system which was to have been bought by the US, but is used by a number of other NATO countries.
Right: Nike-Hercules is backbone of NADGE, but is now being replaced, eventually along with Hawk, by the Patriot.

also replace Hawk, but the latter, now that it has been improved, will remain in service for some years.

Air defense weapons can be used in two ways, for area defense or point defense. The former implies the protection of a formation or unit area of operations, while the latter is for defending a specific target such as a vital bridge on a main supply route, headquarters

or nuclear missile launcher site. One of the major problems in the employment of air defense ground weapons is over IFF. While certainly on the NATO side, the large majority of systems have an IFF capability and are able to interrogate aircraft, there is always the danger that the IFF equipment is malfunctioning. It is also very vulnerable to ECM. Therefore, it is likely in the heat of battle that any aircraft or helicopter, unless positively identified as friendly, will be engaged. In order to safeguard against shooting down friendly aircraft, the NATO practice is to define three states of air defense posture. 'Weapons tight' means that targets may only be engaged on order, while 'weapons hold' indicates that fire can only be opened after positive identification. The third, which is used when the enemy has obtained overwhelming air supremacy and allows any aerial target to be engaged, is 'weapons free'.

The Soviets have an air defense company consisting of four ZSU-23-4 and four SA-9 Gaskin in each tank and motor rifle regiment. At division there is an air defense regiment of five batteries each of four SA-6 Gainful or SA-8 Gecko. At army level there is a complete air defense missile brigade with three battalions. Each has three SA-4 Ganef batteries (three launchers each) and four batteries with six ZSU-23-4 in each. Further missile elements are available at front level. In NATO armies, air defense assets in the immediate battle area tend to be controlled at divisional level. The US corps has Stinger teams down at unit level, and the division also has an air defense artillery battalion with two Sgt York batteries, with eighteen systems in each, and two Chaparral SAM batteries (12 systems per battery). The Germans also control their assets in much the same way. The British, however, split control. Blowpipe teams are controlled at divisional level, but the two Rapier regiments in 1(BR) Corps are held in the Corps Artillery Division. The six batteries are then either sent to support the division or retained to guard vital point and area targets in the rear of the corps area. The high and very high level systems are deployed back in depth in an air defense belt which represents the NATO Air Defense Ground Environment (NADGE).

Locating artillery has a variety of very important roles. Besides obtaining current data on survey and meteorology, which is vital to the accuracy of the

guns, there is also the task of locating enemy artillery and mortars. The US Army is just bringing into service the Firefinder Artillery Locating System, which consists of two advanced phase array radars, one to locate artillery guns and the other mortars. They have the ability to locate a shell or mortar bomb in flight and then backtrack down its trajectory to the fire position. This is the principle behind all locating systems, and they work closely with the counter-battery units, feeding their information through artillery intelligence.

The other area in which locating artillery is involved is battlefield surveillance through the use of RPVs and drones. Drones have been in service for some years, and are essentially missiles which contain a camera. They fly on a preset flight path and then return. Their photographs are developed and the results analyzed in terms of possible targets. With the growing awareness that the land battle is likely to be ever fast moving, there is the danger that drone information will be out of date before it can be used,

and hence the need for 'real time' intelligence. Lockheed are therefore developing an RPV for the US Army. This will have a television camera for surveillance and a laser device for range-finding and target designation, which means that it can also be used in conjunction with aerial weapons systems. It can either fly on a preset course or be controlled by an operator and on return to its base it is recovered using a special net developed by the German firm of Dornier GmbH. Each division will have an RPV unit controlled by the divisional artillery. The Israelis used RPVs very successfully to pinpoint Syrian SAM sites in the Bekaa Valley in Lebanon in 1982, and all nations, including the Soviets, are recognizing their value. A variation is the Remotely Piloted Helicopter (RPH), which is also likely to appear above the battlefield in the next few years.

With the revolutionary technological developments now taking place, artillery is likely to assume an even more dominant role on the battlefield. Indeed, especially in NATO eyes, it could prove decisive in its ability to bring down devastating fire on both hard and soft targets with almost instantaneous response.

Left: Soviet SA-9 Gaskin mounted on BRDM-2.
Below: Canadian Remotely Piloted Helicopter.

7. SPECIAL TO TASK

US 82nd Airborne Division arrives on the battlefield.

Special to task forces are those which are organized and dedicated for particular strategic tasks. NATO has two major forces which come within this context, the ACE Mobile Force, which was mentioned in Chapter 1, and the Rapid Deployment Force (RDF).

The ACE Mobile Force was set up in 1960 to counter threats to the flanks of NATO without being forced to the ultimate step of immediate nuclear retaliation. In many ways it reflects more than anything else the true spirit of Article 5 of the North Atlantic Treaty, which recognizes that an attack on one member nation is an attack on the Alliance as a whole and that each member will 'assist the Party or Parties so attacked by taking forthwith, individually and in concert with other parties, such action as it deems necessary, including the use of armed force, to restore and maintain the security of the North Atlantic area'. In particular, being a multinational force, the ACE Mobile Force provides a clear demonstration of NATO solidarity.

The force has two major elements, land and air. The latter, ACE Mobile Force (Air) (AMF(A)), has no permanent commander or headquarters and when activated it is placed under the control of the Allied Tactical Air Force or Regional Air Commander of the area in which the AMF is deployed. Each nation in the force is responsible for providing its own airlift, although additional assistance is given by the US Military Airlift Command (MAC). The land element, AMF(L), is a permanent standing force, with headquarters at Seckenheim in the FRG and comes directly under SACEUR.

The post of Commander AMF(L) is held in turn by each of the nations involved and is currently a Canadian major general. His headquarters is multinational and no less than seven nations contribute to the force. The Belgians have a battalion of their Parachute Commando Regiment, a 105mm howitzer battery and Milan ATGW company, while the Canadians produce a battalion from their Special Service Force, a 105mm pack howitzer battery and a flight of tactical lift helicopters. The Italian contribution is an Alpini battalion, another 105mm battery and, if required, a field hospital. The Luxembourg element is notable in that it is the whole of her small operational army, the 1st (Light) Infantry Battalion. The Germans produce a heliborne battalion and 105mm battery, hospital and signals company, while the British have an infantry battalion, 105mm battery, CVR(T) reconnaissance squadron, communication elements, and the artillery and logistic headquarters, together with four Puma helicopters. Finally, the US provides another battalion and 105mm battalion, engineer and aviation companies. All elements, apart from the US, which is based in Northern Italy, are located in peacetime on national territory, but, being on light scales the force is quickly deployable.

The most likely areas to which the AMF will be

Far left: US psychological warfare (psywar) team with portable loudspeaker system.
Above: Soviet naval infantry landing from an air cushion vehicle.
Left: US Special Forces team wading a river.
Below: Soviet mountain troops. Because most Soviet training is carried out on open steppes, they consider the closer NATO Central Region terrain as semi-mountainous.

Above: US Special Force soldier with anti-frostbite facial protection.
Above right: Infiltration by water is a special force technique.
Far right: The helicopter is another means of insertion.
Below right: US Special Forces normal temperate climate camouflage.

deployed are Norway, Denmark, Italy, Greece and Turkey. Of particular concern are the maritime choke points, which are very likely Soviet objectives. The decision to deploy the AMF in a period of tension would take place at the very highest NATO level, the North Atlantic Council. If they considered that a show of force was needed to defuse the situation, they would call on the NATO Military Committee to recommend the form it should take. Provided that the member nation under threat agreed, and it was a threat on the flanks, SACEUR would be instructed to deploy the AMF. He would then give orders to the AMF(L) commander, and alert member nations providing the AMF(A) elements, as well as the Regional Air Command involved. AMF(A) would deploy on orders of the latter, while AMF(L) would be placed under AFNORTH or AFSOUTH, who would, as likely as not, delegate operational control to the local command in which the Force was being deployed. It must be emphasized, though, that the AMF is essentially a political deterrent, and that

deploying it will, it is hoped, avert war. If hostilities do break out however, it would be, in spite of its light equipment, a valuable immediate reinforcement for the host nation. Its main problem is its size. If simultaneous crises should appear on both flanks, it is currently not large enough to be deployed to both.

The Middle East oil crisis and Yom Kippur War of 1973 made Western nations realize how dependent they were on oil supplies from the Persian Gulf. The vulnerability of them was further reinforced by the overthrow of the Shah of Iran, the seizing of the US Embassy in Teheran and the holding of many of its members as hostage, as well as by the Soviet intervention in Afghanistan. Until this time, NATO attention had been concentrated firmly on Europe, but it was the US that recognized that threats could be developed against the Alliance elsewhere. The first public announcement of US concern came in President Carter's State of the Union address in 1980 when he warned the Soviet Union and the world in general that 'an attempt by any outside force to gain control of the Persian Gulf region will be repelled by any means necessary including military force'. In order to counter this threat, the Rapid Deployment Joint Task Force (RDJTF, or RDF for short) was set up, with a US Marine Corps general to command it. Initially it was placed under the US Readiness Com-

mand and its strength was envisaged as one Marine and four Army divisions. In fact, it is made up of a Marine Amphibious Force (MAF) with its associated air wing and 7th Marine Amphibious Brigade. The Army elements are spearheaded by the only airborne division remaining in the US inventory, 82nd Airborne Division of three brigades. One of these, the Division Ready Brigade (DRB) is on permanent standby. 101st Airborne Division is now an airmobile formation, equipped with the Black Hawk helicopter, and is also assigned to the RDF. A mechanized infantry division, the 24th, is also available, along with Ranger and Special Force elements. In all the RDF has a strength of 220,000 men, excluding USAF elements.

The main problem is the quick deployment of the force to the Persian Gulf. This would be carried out by MAC's strategic airlift, and ideally men and materiel would be fed in through a friendly airfield in the area. This, however, cannot be guaranteed. Thus the base of Diego Garcia in the Indian Ocean is being used, and the Marines would land here and draw their equipment from ships already prepositioned in the Indian Ocean. Indeed a Marine Task Force is permanently positioned in the Indian Ocean, and this could act as a spearhead, especially since Diego Garcia is some 2400 nautical miles from the Straits of

Hormuz at the entrance to the Gulf. The Marines therefore might well have to lead the way. The other option is for 82nd Airborne Division to carry out a drop in order to seize and secure an airfield.

The RDF is not without its problems. There has been a question mark on its response time, and the placing of it under a new command, US Central Command (USCENTCOM) has shortened the lines of communication between it and the White House. The remoteness of Diego Garcia from the RDF's potential area of operations and the massive airlift resources required to lift the RDF from CONUS mean that it will be some time before a force in reasonable strength will be on the ground. In the meantime, Soviet forces from the Southern TMO might well have seized the Gulf oilfields. There is also concern that the force lacks the weapons to deal with a large armor threat. Although it has ATGW, armor and air support, again it will take time to deploy it, and difficulty in coping with an armored thrust.

There is also a political problem. The RDF is essentially a national US force and is not part of NATO. Its existence and role benefit NATO countries and the US would like material contributions towards it from them. However, this has so far met with a lukewarm response, especially since NATO

Far left: The Red Beret is almost universal as the symbol of airborne forces.
Left: Checking equipment before boarding the aircraft. US and Egyptian parachutists on joint RDF/host nation exercises in Egypt.
Below: RDF Hueycobras over the Pyramids.

European members are finding it difficult enough to maintain their present force levels because of budgetary difficulties. At the same time, the Reagan Administration has called for the force to be increased to over 400,000 men in order to give it more of a global capability. If this is agreed, unless NATO nations are prepared to take over some of the RDF out-of-area commitments in the Middle East or contribute more to the defense of the Central Region, the US might well be forced to withdraw troops from Europe and the gap left might be hard to fill. Another point is that the Army divisions assigned to it also have a NATO reinforcement role, and by the time the RDF begins to deploy, World War III might well have broken out elsewhere, and these formations might be already committed.

Nevertheless, like the AMF, the RDF is essentially a political instrument, designed to deter a would be aggressor by its very existence, and this might be sufficient to prevent an overture to World War III being conducted in an area far removed from NATO's main area of interest.

In terms of spearheads, one of the notable aspects of the initial Soviet operations in Czechoslovakia in 1968 and Afghanistan in 1979 was the use of airborne units. Although they were not used in the parachute role, it was they who initially secured the civil airport at Prague so that further troops could be airlanded, and they were also deployed to Kabul a month before

Left: British paratroops about to board a C-130 Hercules.
Below left: Soviet paratroops attack supported by a BMD MICV.
Above: British and US paratroops prior to a drop.
Below: Canadian paratroops from the Canadian Airborne Regiment.

137

138

Above left: Soviet air assault troops boarding Mi-8 Hips.
Below left: The final check for Soviet paratroops before
boarding an Ilyushin Il-76. It can take 140 men.
Above: Soviet paratroopers in winter camouflage land.

the actual intervention took place. In both cases, the
ground troops then moved across the national
borders and linked up with them. The Soviets have
eight airborne divisions and these are considered an
elite, an indication being that they all have the
'Guards' prefix.

There are two types of airborne troops, the
normal airborne divisions and brigades, and those
organized for long range reconnaissance and operations with partisans. The strategic missions of the
former in general war are the seizure of centers of
government and disruption of attempts to organize
resistance, attacks on key ports and airfields which the
enemy might use to pass reinforcements through,
disruption of major logistic centers and to spearhead
major assaults. At the operational and tactical levels
they would be used to destroy NBC delivery means
and attack reinforcements and headquarters, and in
seizing key demolitions and bridges and other points
which would facilitate the advance of the ground
forces. Soviet airborne divisions are organized on a
triangular basis with three airborne infantry regiments, each of three battalions of approximately 450
men each. What is particularly impressive is the
range of weapons systems found. The airborne
battalion is equipped with the BMD MICV, armed
like the BMP with a 73mm smoothbore gun and
Sagger ATGW, along with a separate ATGW
platoon and 82mm mortar platoon. At regimental

level there is an ATGW company, antitank gun
company with six 85mm M-45 antitank guns, an
artillery battery with six 122mm howitzers or 120mm
mortars and an air defense company with towed twin
23mm ZSU-23 guns. The Division also has a battalion
of ASU-85 assault guns, with three companies of ten
guns each, a BRDM reconnaissance battalion, an
airborne rocket launcher battalion with the RPU-14
140mm sixteen tube MRLS and an air defense
battalion with eighteen further twin ZSU-23-2 guns.
To transport them, heavy lift aircraft, including the
An-12, An-22 and Il-76, the Soviet equivalents to the
US C-130 and C-5, and it is reckoned that there
is sufficient first line lift to carry up to three divisions
on light scales to a maximum range of 1000km. In
order to maintain an airborne force, especially in
out-of-area operations, aircraft of the state airline
Aeroflot would be used, but would have to be converted. The Soviets have claimed to be able to drop a
complete airborne division in the space of 30 minutes
and, if this is so, it would be an ideal way of seizing
control of a vital area such as the Skagerrak or
Dardanelles at the outset of war. Certainly with the
weaponry which they have, they could hold for some
time until reinforcements arrived.

Apart from the airborne divisions themselves, the
Soviets have also introduced air assault brigades,
which are made up of two light infantry battalions
and two BMD battalions and are equipped with
helicopters. They are likely to be placed under command of a front headquarters for a particular operation, the most likely being in conjunction with an

OMG. In this case they would be used to seize and hold vital ground such as bridges over a major water obstacle, and the OMG would then link up with them. It is known that GSFG has an air assault brigade.

The second type of Soviet airborne troops comes more under the special forces category and will be covered later in the chapter. As a final point on 'conventional' airborne troops, it should be noted that the Poles have an airborne division, although not as well equipped as those of the Soviets, and the Czechs have an airborne regiment, as does Rumania and Bulgaria. The Hungarians have an airborne battalion.

NATO places very much less emphasis on airborne forces than the Warsaw Pact. As has been described already, the US has one division, but this is very much part of the RDF, although it could be deployed to Europe. The British airborne element is retained in 5th Infantry Brigade based in the UK, but this is dedicated specifically to out-of-area operations. The Germans have three airborne brigades, but they are being used more and more for airmobile operations with helicopters. Indeed, the airmobile concept which was developed by the French in Algeria and the US in Vietnam is now considered to have very much more relevance to the Central Region than airborne operations, which would, in any event, be difficult to mount in a hostile air environment. Heliborne troops can react very much more quickly and hence are very much more effective in defense. In particular, they can provide quick reaction forces to deal with Soviet airborne and helicopter operations, as well as counter-penetration against OMGs. There is no doubt that NATO is now placing increasing emphasis on airmobile forces, and an indication of this is that one British brigade in the Central Region has recently been converted into this role on a year's trial. Where airborne operations might prove more advantageous to NATO are on the flanks, especially the Southern, where the distances involved are often too great for helicopters to be used. Hence NATO will not disregard airborne troops as part of its overall order of battle for the future.

Another Soviet combat force which must be taken into account is the Naval Infantry, equivalent to the Marines. Here the threat is specifically on the flanks. The Soviet Baltic Fleet has two Naval Infantry brigades, the Northern Fleet and Black Sea Fleet a further two each, while a seventh is with the Pacific Fleet. These are trained in amphibious operations and although their equipment is generally obsolescent, the PT-76 amphibious tank and BTR-60PB being their main vehicles, and are on light scales, they nevertheless do provide a threat. An amphibious assault behind the forward defenses in Norway, the seizure of the Danish islands, or even a diversionary attack on the German or Dutch coast well in the rear of the Central Region would cause NATO problems.

Special Forces, as opposed to Special to task forces, are those designed to operate covertly behind the enemy's lines. The Soviet version of these is known as the *Spetsnaz* or *Reydoviki*. They come under Soviet Military Intelligence, the GRU, and have two basic roles, reconnaissance and sabotage. They are organized into brigades, with probably seven such in existence, one being stationed at Neuruppen in East Germany. The normal distribution being one brigade per front. While for administrative purposes the brigades are broken down into battalions, in wartime the *Spetsnaz* would operate in independent companies, some being placed under army control. Each company is 40–50 strong, which is broken down into six patrols. Others, however, may be as much as 80–100 men and are equipped with recoilless antitank guns and mortars. They will be used more for seizing and holding key points, either to cause disruption or in direct support of the main thrust. While both types will normally be inserted by parachute, although some may well be infiltrated into enemy territory before hostilities begin, the reconnaissance/sabotage patrols will establish covert bases, either in deep woods or even in buildings arranged by fifth columnists. Reconnaissance will be directed at locating missile sites, headquarters, signals centers and logistic installations. These may well be attacked by the sabotage squads, who will also be used to disrupt main supply routes by ambushing resupply convoys, blowing up bridges and the like. Key NATO commanders and politicians may also be targetted, and in this the *Spetsnaz* will work in close cooperation with the KGB. Another tactic which they are very likely to employ is dressing up in NATO uniforms. The Ardennes 1944 counteroffensive is an example of just how disruptive this can be. They will play on the nerves of NATO troops, especially those in logistic units, whose cohesiveness is unlikely to be as strong as those in combat and combat support roles. The task of those involved in rear area security therefore becomes that much more vital. The satellite armies also have their own special forces, which are very much under Soviet control, and most notable are the East German 5th 'Rudi Saenger' and 40th Airborne Battalions.

NATO, of course, has its own Special Forces, and notable among these are the US Special Forces, the Green Berets, who have now been organized into the 1st Special Force Brigade and the British Special Air Service (SAS). The operations in the Falklands in 1982 gave a very good idea of what the SAS *modus operandi* is, and it is likely that they, the Green Berets, and other similar NATO units will carry out the same type of operation.

Operating in four man parties, they will pass back information, especially likely artillery targets, carry out raids and acts of sabotage. It is unlikely, however, that they will follow the *Spetsnaz* example of operating in enemy uniforms since this is against the Geneva Convention. They could be inserted by parachute, using freefall techniques, but it is more likely that they will establish themselves in hides at the outset and let the battle sweep over them.

Soviet airborne and Naval Infantry formations will probably be employed *en masse* more on the NATO flanks than in the Central Region, but both sides will make increasing use of heliborne troops, which will speed up the tempo of the battle even more than at present. Special Forces will also be employed and might well have an effect out of all proportion to their limited numbers. The employment of all these types of specialist force make the need for effective rear area security paramount.

Above: The BMD gives Soviet airborne and air assault troops added punch.
Below: US paratroops consolidate the dropping zone (DZ).

8. AIR SUPPORT

General Dynamics F-16 Fighting Falcon air combat fighter in Royal Netherlands Air Force colors.

The military theorists of the 1920s believed that air power on its own could win wars through its ability to strike at the very heart of the enemy. World War II showed this to be mistaken, but also demonstrated how much air supremacy could influence the land battle, both in terms of preventing enemy air from operating against friendly ground forces and giving active support through attacks on enemy ground forces and the provision of air lift.

Air operations in war are strategic or tactical. Strategic operations are concerned mainly with strikes, nuclear and conventional, deep into enemy territory and their effect on the land battle is only indirect. Tactical air operations, however, are of direct concern to the ground troops, and can be considered in three broad categories – air transport operations, counter air and offensive air support. All three can involve fixed wing and rotary aircraft. As a general rule, although there are exceptions, fixed wing operations are the responsibility of air forces, while helicopters are manned and controlled by armies. Fixed wing operations will be considered first.

Fixed wing air transport operations have been covered to an extent in the previous chapter. They cover the transport of troops and materiel within a theater of operations. This includes airborne and airlanding operations, resupply by air and the evacuation of casualties. The last two roles will be considered in Chapter Ten. Enough has been said about airborne operations. Two examples of airlanding operations were the deployment of Soviet airborne forces to Prague in 1968 and Kabul in 1979. The RDF would also hope to carry out this type of operation if a friendly airport close to the projected area of operations could be found. As far as the Central Region is concerned, however, this type of operation is most unlikely to take place apart from bringing in reinforcements into the theater.

As far as the air forces are concerned, the counter air battle is crucial. It is defined as gaining and maintaining a favorable air situation and preventing the enemy from interfering effectively with land, air and sea operations. The battle can take two forms, defensive and offensive. In the former it is fought in the air in the air space which is required to give effective support to the ground forces, and is essentially a battle of attrition. Alternatively, attacks are made on enemy airfields with the object of destroying his aircraft on the ground as well as his fuel stocks and maintenance facilities. A classic example of this is the Israeli preemptive strike on Egyptian airfields at the outset of the 1967 war.

Unless the counter air battle is won, and it may take some time, offensive air support for the ground forces will be difficult to carry out. Nevertheless, the two will be carried out simultaneously, but the ground forces will not have all their demands met until success has been achieved in the counter air battle. Offensive air support itself is made up of four distinct types of operation. The first, close air support is air action against hostile targets close to friendly forces which requires detailed integration with the fire and movement of those forces. Its effects, however, are often only very local and in terms of limited air assets air forces regard this as a lower priority than other types. Interdiction is designed to impede or restrict the movement of enemy forces, reinforcements and supplies into and within the battlefield. Interdiction targets will normally be beyond the range of ground weapons, and the most profitable ones are supply routes, communications centers, bridges and troop concentrations. A favorable air very much more far reaching, although this will not be immediately apparent to the forward troops.

The other two types of operation both involve reconnaissance. Armed reconnaissance is used to describe missions flown to attack targets of opportunity. The pilot has a roving commission over a particular area, which might be over the immediate battlefield itself, in which case it can be considered as close air support, or further forward, in which case it is a form of interdiction. Finally, tactical air reconnaissance is that flown which provides information which might influence the immediate battle. This is opposed to strategic air reconnaissance carried out at high level by such aircraft as the TR-1.

There are four ways in which information can be obtained from tactical air reconnaissance. Day and night optical photography is one, and cameras have now been developed to cater for low level, high speed and low light photographs. With good photographic interpreters a mass of information can be gleaned from photographs, but the results take time to be processed and by the time that they are, it may be too late to act on them. Visual observation is more responsive, but, normally carried out at very low level, it is a difficult and highly specialized task, especially when the modern high speed reconnaissance aircraft will cross a target a mile long in eight seconds. Visual reconnaissance can either cover the detailed search of an area to build up a comprehensive picture of enemy activity, be a search along roads, railways, waterways and other lines of communication, or be directed against a particular point, usually to confirm information obtained from other sources. Normally a pilot will give an inflight report while he is still airborne, and then be debriefed in detail once he has landed. To help him, the aircraft is often fitted with a recorder, enabling him to give a running commentary during the course of his mission. Obviously, visual reconnaissance is limited to

Above left: Su-17 Fitter C, a typical Soviet counterair aircraft which can be used for ground attack.
Left: Su-7 Fitter, still the backbone of TMO ground support aviation.

Left: Close Air Support—Artist's impression of US
A-10s breaking up a Soviet tank attack.
Above: USAF F-4G can carry a variety of weapons fits
and is well suited to interdiction tasks.

conditions of good visibility.

Infrared Linescan (IRLS) operates on the television principle and, using infrared enables it to penetrate foliage and some camouflage. The final type is radar reconnaissance, involving the use of both forward looking radar and SLAR. Radar, although it has nothing like the resolution of photography, has advantages in not being weather dependent, has wider and therefore quicker cover, and gives the pilot greater tactical freedom in that he does not have to fly in a straight line.

NATO tactical air support in the Central Region is provided through 2 and 4 ATAF. The former is made up of elements of the Belgian, British, Dutch and German air forces, while 4 ATAF has Canadian, US and German aircraft. National air elements are not tied to supporting their own ground forces, but will operate in support of each army group as a whole. Thus a mission in support of VII(US) Corps is just as likely to be carried out by Canadian or German aircraft as US. Within 4 ATAF the following types of aircraft are used:

USAF – A-10, F-4C, F-4D, F-4E, F-4G,
F-15C, F-16A, F-111E fighter/attack, RF-4C
reconnaissance
RCAF – CF-5 fighter/attack
Luftwaffe – F-4F, Alphajet, Tornado IDS
fighter/attack, RF-4E reconnaissance

In 2 ATAF are found:

Belgian Air Force – F-16AB, Mirage
VBA/BD fighter attack, Mirage VBR
reconnaissance
Luftwaffe – as above
RNAF – F-16A/B, NF-5A/B fighter attack
NF-104G reconnaissance
RAF – Phantom (F-4), Buccaneer, Jaguar,
Harrier, Tornado IDS fighter/attack, with
Jaguar also being used for reconnaissance.

In all, NATO could expect to field some 2700 aircraft in the Central Region.

Left: This Royal Canadian Air Force F-18 will be fighting
the counterair battle.
Below: The US A-10 is subsonic and specifically designed
for ground attack.

The air force supporting the Warsaw Pact TMO is divided into three departments. The first covers ground support, and in it are found regiments and divisions of Su-7 Fitter, MiG-21 Fishbed, Su-17 C, D and H Fitter and MiG-27 Flogger D. The counter-air department will have MiG-21 Fishbed C, D and F, Su-17 Fitter C, D, H and MiG-23 Flogger, while the military aviation department would look after helicopter and light transport assets. In addition, this air force will also have available to it five Su-24 Fencer regiments of the 24th Air Army, which is now part of the Aviation Armies of the Soviet Union (AASU) and looks after all strategic aircraft. In all, the TMO will have some 3600 aircraft available to it.

Both NATO and the Warsaw Pact believe in control of fixed wing air assets at the highest possible level. Indeed, the Soviets, by removing this control from the fronts, who used to have one frontal aviation air army each, to the TMO, do so at a higher level than NATO. Because modern combat aircraft are capable of carrying out a number of roles and are as effective in counterair as offensive air support and because there are always going to be more demands than there are aircraft available, it is logical that control should remain at the highest level.

Air support missions are either preplanned or immediate. Normally counter air, interdiction and reconnaissance are the former, while close air support is immediate. The former are passed up through the chain of command and, unless a specific number of sorties has been allocated to a particular formation, in which case it will make the decision to accept or reject, they are considered at the highest level. In the NATO chain of command this would be by the Joint Command Operations Center (JCOC) which is situated at the joint ATAF/Army Group headquarters. The air element of this, the Air Command Operations Center (ACOC), then tasks the aircraft for the mission. If the request is an immediate one, it is passed immediately back to the ACOC, and the air commander will keep a certain number of sorties available for this. In order to give a quick response, the pilot is already in the aircraft ready to go, and can be briefed in as little as two or three minutes, and will be airborne in about five. Another method is for the aircraft to orbit a holding point near the battle area, the 'cab rank' system as used in World War II. When his fuel runs low, he can be relieved by another aircraft or be refueled from a tanker aircraft. Although the response time is very fast, it is very uneconomic and would only be used in exceptional circumstances, such as an enemy breakthrough.

The responsibility for deciding the weapons to be used on a mission rests with the air commander, and there is a wide range available, depending on the nature of the target. The World War II type of iron bomb is still used. The USAF has four weights – 250lb, 500lb, 1000lb and 2000lb – and these have variable fuses. They can thus be used for attacks on bridges and roads, and also, with the fuse set to air burst, against troop concentrations and soft skinned vehicles. They are usually dropped at low level and many types now have a retarding tail device to prevent them bouncing off the target or damaging the aircraft in the blast. A more sophisticated type is the stand off bomb, which enables the aircraft to release it out of range of the air defense weapons protecting the target. Known as 'smart bombs', these were used extensively in Vietnam with much success against point targets such as bridges. A number of guidance systems can be used, and examples are the Paveway family of laser guided bombs in the US service and the Walleye TV glide bomb. Cluster Bomb Units (CBU) are widespread and contain antiarmor and antipersonnel submunitions, and can be used as a means of dispensing chemical agents. Against hardened targets like runways, bunkers and aircraft shelters another family of air delivered munitions exists. The idea behind these is that they should penetrate to a certain depth before exploding. Examples of these are the Soviet BETAB-500, which is a rocket-propelled bomb, the British JP-233 system, dispensing submunitions, which are a mixture of concrete penetrating and antipersonnel, the latter to hinder repair work, and the US Tomahawk Airfield Attack Munition (TAAM). Unguided rockets are also employed extensively. The Soviets use the S-55 55mm in pods containing 8, 16, 19 or 32 rockets, but also have 137mm, 190mm and 212mm rockets which are hung individually under the aircraft. NATO air forces use smaller calibers and the 2.75in is the most popular in a pod of 7 or 19 rockets. They are usually employed against armor, but can be fragmentation or smoke. Cannon are mounted on all aircraft and can be of the Gatling type, like the 20mm Vulcan, which can fire 6000 rounds per minute, or the more conventional single barrel. Calibers range from 20mm to 30mm.

The final category is the air-to-surface missile (ASM) which is guided. On the Soviet side, the most likely type to be seen on or near the battlefield is the AS-7 Kerry, which is radio guided and has a range of 10km. It is carried by both the Su-17 and Su-24. The latter also carries other ASMs, designated AS-9 (antiradiation), AS-10 (television guidance), AS-11 (television guidance with data link) and AS-12 (antiradiation). Antiradiation missiles, which home onto radar emissions are particularly ideal against air defense targets. NATO equivalents are Martel, Shrike and Standard. A more general purpose ASM is the Hughes AGM-65 Maverick, with a range of over 20km which uses television, laser or infrared guidance.

Above: A US F-4 releasing a GBU-15 precision guided or 'smart' glide bomb.
Right: A Royal Danish Air Force F-16 armed with AIM-9L air-to-air Sidewinder missiles.

When used in the close support role, the aircraft relies on a ground controller, known as a Forward Air Controller (FAC), to guide him onto the target. He does this by talking the pilot down by radio and will use smoke to mark the target if it is obscure. This generally works well, but FACs in future are more likely to use laser designators to mark the target, and laser guided munitions will be used, homing in on the laser reflection off the target.

Both 'smart' bombs and ASMs are Precision Guided Munitions, and it is the rapid developments in these which are giving NATO the air capability to strike at the Warsaw Pact 2nd echelon forces, especially as with increasing ranges it is possible to fire them from behind friendly lines, using RPVs to designate the target. This is the air contribution envisaged in Airland 2000, along with aerial surveillance devices designed to give 'real time' information on the enemy.

World War III will initially be dominated in the air by the counter air battle, which will be one between sophistication on one side and numbers on the other. Below this battle Warsaw Pact tactical air will be carrying out tactical reconnaissance, supporting ground thrusts through attacks on NATO ground defenses, attacking reserves and disrupting the rear areas. In particular, close air support will be used, along with artillery to pave the way for the OMG or raids by forward detachments. NATO tactical air reconnaissance will be much concerned in locating the 2nd echelon so that it can be attacked, but during the opening days of the war there will also be heavy demands on close air support to help offset numerical inferiority in the frontline. With threats from both air and ground, attrition rates on both sides are likely to be high until one side gains air supremacy.

While the opposing forces are engaged in what is likely to be a desperate battle, the helicopter will also be very busy. There are five types of military helicopter. The smallest is the light helicopter used for reconnaissance, liaison, fire direction and limited exercise of command. The US Bell OH-58 Kiowa, the French Gazelle and the German MBB BO 105, all of which are in NATO service, are good examples. The Soviets do not have this type, although it is possible that they may be developing a model. They do, however, have a wide range of utility helicopters, which are designed for troop and logistic lift of limited load, especially the Mi-2 Hoplite and Mi-4 Hound, and use these for reconnaissance as well. In the NATO armory this type is reflected by the Sikorsky UH-60 Black Hawk and the British Westland Lynx. The third type is the heavy lift or support helicopter, of which, in western eyes, the most famous and widely used is the Boeing CH-47 Chinook, which can take up to 44 troops up to 115 miles. The Soviet Mi-8 Hip will take 28 troops twice this range, but the Mi-26 Halo carries some 90 troops 500 miles.

Previous page: US F-15s taking off from a makeshift airstrip which is under enemy attack.
Above: RAF Puma lifting a 105mm light gun. The helicopter is invaluable used with artillery like this in difficult terrain.
Below: Typical Soviet helicopters in service today.
Above right: The Soviet Mi-26 Halo can carry 90 troops or over 40,000lbs of stores and equipment.
Below right: Soviet Mi-24 Hind attack helicopters, which have made a deep impression on NATO.

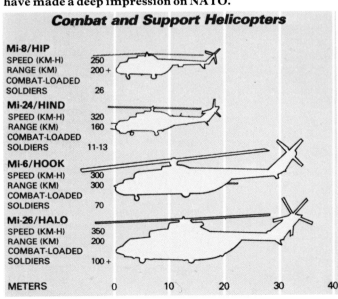

Combat and Support Helicopters

Mi-8/HIP
SPEED (KM-H) 250
RANGE (KM) 200 +
COMBAT-LOADED
SOLDIERS 26

Mi-24/HIND
SPEED (KM-H) 320
RANGE (KM) 160
COMBAT-LOADED
SOLDIERS 11-13

Mi-6/HOOK
SPEED (KM-H) 300
RANGE (KM) 300
COMBAT-LOADED
SOLDIERS 70

Mi-26/HALO
SPEED (KM-H) 350
RANGE (KM) 200
COMBAT-LOADED
SOLDIERS 100 +

METERS   0   10   20   30   40

Above: Technician examining the nose-mounted sight on an AH-1 Hueycobra.
Left: Mi-24 Hind D engaging tanks with rockets and AT-2 Swatter ATGW (artist's impression).

The above types of helicopter are unarmed in their basic configuration, but when they have weapons installed, they become known as armed helicopters. Thus the Gazelle, which is used by the British Army has been turned into an armed helicopter by installation of ATGW, and the Soviet Hip is also often found equipped with rocket pods and/or ATGW. The most formidable helicopter on the battlefield is, however, the attack helicopter, which is specifically designed as an armed helicopter, with permanently fitted sights and weapon systems. The first of these to appear was the Bell Hueycobra, which performed excellent service in Vietnam, but is now being partially replaced by the Hughes AH-64 Apache. The Soviet version is the Mi-24 Hind.

The armament carried by the armed or attack helicopter comes in three basic types. Both the Apache and the Hind-D have a cannon, the 30mm Hughes Chain Gun and a 12.7mm Gatling respectively. This is an ideal weapon against light armored vehicles. The Hind also, can mount four rocket pods each containing 32 S-55 rockets, as can the Hueycobra, which has 2.75in rocket pods. A variant of this weapons configuration is the 40mm grenade launcher

Left: Soviet Mi-6 Hook carrying a tractor as an underslung load.
Above: Falklands 1982 – Royal Marines board a Wessex helicopter for a quick redeployment.

on the Hueycobra; however, while useful in counter-insurgency operations in Vietnam, it is seldom used in Northwest Europe, and the Apache does not have this. The most significant armament on attack helicopters is, however, ATGW, which enables them to become very effective tank killers. Indeed, after NATO trials in Europe in the late Sixties and successes by the US against North Vietnamese tanks in 1972, a school grew up believing that the helicopter alone was more than a match for a main battle tank and hence the latter's days were numbered. Moderation prevailed, however, but it was recognized that the ATGW helicopter was a valuable addition to the family of antiarmor weapons. The Hind can mount four ATGW launchers, Sagger being the most usual, although the latest model, the Hind-E, has a new ATGW system, the AT-6 Spiral. The Hueycobra can carry eight TOW missiles, while the Apache is able to mount up to sixteen Rockwell Hellfire missiles. The Hellfire has been designed specifically for attack helicopters and is laser guided, either by means of an airborne or ground laser designator. It

has a range of 7km and consists of two shaped charge warheads in tandem, which can penetrate the thickest tank frontal armor likely to exist before the turn of the century. NATO European member helicopters are all armed, as opposed to attack, but mount TOW, HOT and Swingfire ATGW.

Soviet helicopters are organized into flights of four, and at divisional level there are one or two flights of Hind, one of Hip and one of Hoplite. Backing this up at army level are a further four or five Hind flights, three or four of Hip and three or four of Hoplite. They are manned by the army, but when operating with ground troops will be controlled by an air force FAC. During the attack, the Soviets see the armed and attack helicopter as a good means of covering open flanks and of providing additional fire-power, especially in the event of an enemy counter-attack. They will also operate in the depth of the enemy's defenses and contain his reserves. Their targets will be armor, ATGW and air defense systems.

In conjunction with fixed wing aviation, the Soviets see the helicopter as an important adjunct to the operations of an OMG or raiding force. While the air assault brigade will operate with the OMG at the operational level, there is a need for attack, utility and C³ helicopters to accompany the OMG, especially in

A Hughes AH-64 Apache attack helicopter firing Hellfire ATGW. Note how it uses the cover of the trees, making it a difficult target.

helping to clear its path and in reconnaissance. Normally, they will travel with the OMG, setting up their own landing zones (LZ) as they go, but if the OMG is still operating close to the main forces and the enemy air defenses have been well suppressed, then they will operate from within friendly territory. Both OMGs and raiding groups are likely to employ heliborne operations, but the Soviets consider that the ground force must link up with the heliborne elements within six hours, since the latter will not have sufficient heavy weapons to hold out for longer. In general, Soviet helicopters operate much more closely with fixed wing assets than NATO's.

The US division has, besides the air cavalry troop within the armored cavalry squadron, an aviation company. This is mainly to provide the commander with C³ assets and consists of six observation and four utility helicopters. Each brigade headquarters also has four light helicopters and the divisional artillery has a further nine, together with

Above: A British Army Lynx armed helicopter with pintle mounted 7.62mm in doorway and, below, pod mounted twin 7.62mm machine guns.
Right: French troops deploy from Aerospatiale's AS 332B Super Puma.

two utility. Thus, in total, the division has nine attack, 36 light and 14 utility helicopters, which is considerably more than its Soviet counterpart. However, within the Division 86 organization, each US division in Germany is to have its helicopter assets dramatically boosted by the addition of a cavalry air attack brigade. This will consist of two ground cavalry troops, each with 19 Bradley M3s and three mortars, two air cavalry troops (six light and four attack helicopters each) and two helicopter attack battalions. These will be organized into three attack helicopter companies, each with four scout and seven attack helicopters. The prime role of the brigade will be the destruction of enemy armor. As for heavy lift helicopters, these are retained in the corps aviation battalion. As one of the exceptions to the general rule that fixed wing aircraft are an air force responsibility, the US Army has the Grumman OV-1 Mohawk, which is used mainly for reconnaissance and electronic warfare.

The Continental European NATO members tend to concentrate their helicopter assets at corps level, although the Germans have a light helicopter company in each division. The British, however, provide the other exception to the general rule in that their heavy lift helicopters are an air force responsibility. As for the other types, these are organized into regiments (equivalent to a US battalion), one to each division and one as corps troops. Each regiment consists of two squadrons each of 12 helicopters. One is equipped with Gazelle, with reconnaissance as its main role, while the other has Lynx, fitted as an armed helicopter with TOW and ATGW. The experimental airmobile brigade is likely to result in some reorganization of helicopter assets, with the RAF heavy lift helicopters in Germany being dedicated to this brigade. It is also likely that it will have a squadron permanently detached from one of the Army Air Corps regiments.

In terms of the antiarmor battle, the NATO concept of operations for the armed and attack helicopters is that they should be held back initially, apart from giving assistance in the covering force battle. Because they are very flexible and highly responsive weapons, they are ideal for countering a sudden breakthrough, and this is what they will be kept for, especially in the OMG context. Attack helicopters normally operate with light helicopters. The latter locates the target and then directs the attack helicopter onto it. Both will hug the ground closely, using covered approaches, thus making a very fleeting target to the enemy.

It is clear that the helicopter, with its obvious advantages as a weapons platform, is playing an increasingly important role on the battlefield. In the past it has been limited by the problems of operating in bad weather and at night, but improved avionics are eradicating these. The next generation, as represented by the US Light Helicopter Experimental (LHX) program, which will see current types replaced by an attack/scout and utility version, will be smaller, lighter, more powerful and with much greater survivability. Rather than avoiding enemy defenses, they will be more prepared to take them on directly, relying on high speed and 'fire and forget' weapons. A new role is also about to appear, that of the anti-helicopter helicopter, which might well mean that there will in future be two counter air battles, fixed wing and, much closer to the ground, rotary wing.

9. ENGINEERS

US Corps of Engineers bridging boat.

The overall role of the combat engineers in war is to improve the mobility of their own troops, while impeding that of the enemy's. Their tasks are therefore neatly divided into mobility and countermobility.

Mobility tasks are mainly concerned with the improvement of routes which combat troops wish to use. They cover improvements to roads and tracks, the overcoming of natural obstacles such as rivers and streams, the clearing of artificial obstacles, including minefields, and the construction, maintenance and repair of airlanding facilities for fixed and rotary wing aircraft. Countermobility, on the other hand, includes route denial to the enemy by demolition, mining and cratering, the preparation of obstacles, artificial and the enhancement of natural obstacles and the destruction of logistic installations to prevent them falling into enemy hands. In order to carry out these tasks a wide range of equipment is needed.

In order to put these tasks in their proper context, it is simplest to describe the role of the engineer as the battle unfolds. Once NATO has made the decision to deploy its troops in the Central Region, the engineers will be especially busy. Because detailed plans are already drawn up, they will be well aware of their tasks and engineer units will have been allocated to them. Almost all NATO armies have an engineer battalion in each division, with further support at corps level, and Warsaw Pact forces have a similar organization, except that each tank and motor rifle regiment also has an engineer company. The first task of NATO engineers will be to put the barrier plan into effect. This is the overall construction plan for obstacles which each corps has.

First and foremost is the laying of minefields. There are five different kinds. Protective minefields are those laid close to a defensive position, normally just out of grenade range, and are often put down by the unit itself. Nuisance minefields are self-explanatory, and are scattered groups of mines laid to disrupt the enemy. Ideal sites are approaches to bridges, around roadblocks, ferry sites and fords. Defensive minefields are more extensive and are laid as part of the overall tactical plan in order to disorganize and delay the enemy by breaking up his attacks. They are always covered by direct and indirect fire weapons. Barrier minefields are usually the largest and are placed to deny the enemy entry into a particular piece of terrain. They are often combined with a natural obstacle and again covered by fire. The final type is the phoney minefield, which is marked as a minefield, but has no mines laid.

Mines are either antitank or antipersonnel and minefields normally consist of a mixture of both. The basic type of antitank mine is the heavy handlaid

**Left: A British Barmine layer towed by an FV432 APC.
Above: The oblong Barmines are fed into the chute of the
layer enabling an antitank minefield to be rapidly laid.**

type which relies on blast to destroy the tracks and
suspension of the tank, and is represented by the
US M15 antitank mine, the Soviet TM-46 and the
British Mk 7. They are usually fitted with antihandling devices. A heavier version is the US M21
heavy antitank mine which has a shaped charge
effect, producing a self-forging fragment and this is
known as the Misznay-Schardin effect. These are all
metallic mines and can be easily detected. In order
to make them more difficult to locate all-plastic mines
have now been introduced including the US M19
Antitank mine. Another type of antiarmor device is
the Off-Route Antitank Mine (ORATM). Here a
pressure tape is placed across the route and when an
AFV crosses over it, a hollow charge projectile is
launched from the side of the road, hitting the vehicle
in the side. The US uses the M24 and the British,
the French MIACAH (Mine Antichar à Action
Horizontale) system. The US is also developing a
new system which replaces the tell-tale tape with an
acoustic sensor and infrared fuse. A further type of
antitank mine is the British Barmine, with an un-
conventional oblong shape, which has been designed
this way for speed of laying.

The main antipersonnel mine used by NATO
armies is the US Claymore mine. It was originally
developed by the US as a defensive weapon against
enemy infiltration and mass attack and consists of a
container with 700 steel balls, which, when detonated
using a trip wire or electrical impulse, fires the balls
over a 60° arc. They are lethal up to 50m range. The
Soviet OZM3 works on a similar principle. The
Soviets also still use a number of wooden mines, both
antitank and antipersonnel, which, although hard to
detect and cheap to produce, cannot be laid using
mechanical means.

The manual laying of minefields is a time consuming business, and several mechanical laying
systems are now in service. The Soviet PMR-3 is a
two-wheel trailer with plough incorporated, and is
normally towed behind a modified BTR-152 wheeled
APC and can lay mines at a rate of 4–6km per hour.
The US Ground-Emplaced Mine-Scattering Systems
(GEMSS) lays 4lb antitank surface mines and is a
trailer, like the PMR-3, and can lay a 2500m minefield,
which will consist of several rows, in much less time
than the 50 hours using M15 and M21 mines.
The mine itself has a magnetic influence and can be
set for deactivation after a certain period so that
friendly troops can move across the area. The British
and Germans also use the Barmine layer, again
similar to PMR-3 and GEMSS. While GEMSS also

lays antipersonnel mines, the British and Germans use the Ranger for this type. This is a multibarrel projector system normally mounted on an APC. It has 72 disposable tubes, each with 18 antipersonnel mines, which have been specially designed for the system. A tube is launched every second, and the 18 mines in it are randomly distributed up to a range of 100m, being automatically armed 20 seconds after launch. When laying a minefield the Barmine layer and Ranger will operate together.

Both the US and Soviets also lay mines using helicopters, but the latest development in mine warfare is the remotely delivered mine (RDM), fired by artillery or MRLS. The US Army has combined GEMSS with its Family of Scatterable Mines (FASCAM) program. This is designed to lay down hasty minefields in order to canalize the enemy into areas where he will present a good target. While conventional minefields have the disadvantage that they can impede the defender's mobility as well as that of the attacker, FASCAM has much more flexibility and fits in much better with the highly mobile battle which the US Army expects to fight in the future.

Defensive minefields will be laid with clear lanes running through them so that the covering forces in front of them are able to get back through when the

time for withdrawal comes. NATO doctrine considers the control of these and key bridges which have been set for demolition as very important. Indeed, history is littered with examples of bridges being blown too early, thus trapping friendly forces on the wrong side of the river, or too late, enabling the enemy to capture it intact. A classic example of the latter was the Remagen Bridge over the Rhine, which the US 9th Armored Division captured in March 1945 and cost the life of the German officer in charge in front of a firing squad. The basic principles of reserved demolitions are that control over them is kept at the highest level for as long as possible and that there must be sufficient force to defend them against enemy surprise attack. It is also necessary for all concerned to have accurate information on the troops likely to pass back through the reserve demolition and monitor their progress. As the battle gets closer, so the power to authorize the firing of the demolition is passed down the chain of command and normally ends up with the demolition guard commander, who will give the engineer firing party the order. Special forms are used so that there can be no confusion over the instructions, and these are standard throughout all NATO armies.

The Soviets are faced with a mine clearance problem before they even cross the border since they

must clear lanes through the minefields which run the length of the IGB and Czech-German borders. In order not to sacrifice surprise, these mines will be removed some time before hostilities break out. Indeed, some mines were lifted by East German border guards in 1983. Once across the border, however, the problem becomes much more severe. The simplest form of detection device is the probe which, in view of the non-metallic mine, is still widely used. For metallic mines, metal detectors are used. Often, though, it will only be when the first vehicle has blown up that the unit will know that it has come across mines. Engineer reconnaissance, which will be up with the leading troops, must then identify the extent of the minefield.

The basic method of minefield clearance is by hand, but it is very time consuming, especially in dealing with mines equipped with antihandling devices. Since, for the Soviets, speed is of the essence, this method will be seldom used. Instead they will attempt to 'storm' the minefield with engineers leading the attack, while artillery and armor attempt to suppress the enemy fire. Smoke will also be used to provide cover. As a quick way of blowing lanes, the Soviets use hose charges. These are in 500m rigid lengths and are either winched over the minefield or

Far left: British Combat Engineer Tractor towing the Giant Viper minefield clearance device.
Left: British entrenching machine.
Below: Soviet BTM Trencher. It can remove 600–800m^3 of earth per hour.

pushed by tanks. The former is either done by means of a pulley or by means of a rocket propelled grapnel. Another method is to lay it across the minefield with an explosive charge. A better and more effective method is to use a flexible hose, which comes coiled in a box and can be fired from a tank or APC. Both the US and British have similar systems in the M-1 and Giant Viper. The main drawbacks are that the hose is much shorter than the rigid one and the rocket propulsion system is not totally reliable. Indeed, there have been incidents where the hose has wrapped itself round the turret of the tank detonating it and blown it off. The other method, especially when there is not sufficient covering fire available, is to use tanks equipped with ploughs or plough-roller combinations, but this still requires engineers to follow them up as they can only clear an imperfect lane, often missing some mines. Interestingly, the British and US developed many such systems in World War II, which were generally ignored afterwards. The mine threat in Vietnam forced the US Army to reintroduce them, and the US formations in Germany are now equipped with

Left: British sappers prepare a makeshift landing strip.
Below left: British Combat Engineer Tractor carrying trackway, often vitally important for maintaining bank entry and exit trafficability during river crossings.
Below: Launching a pontoon section of a Soviet PMP floating bridge.

AFV mine clearance devices.

There are other types of barrier or obstacle which can and will be constructed. One of the more traditional ones is the antitank ditch. This can be constructed using explosives and plant equipment. The Soviets also have a trench digging and ditching system. An antitank ditch can be surmounted in a number of ways. One is by dropping fascines made up of pieces of wood bound together in a large roll, an old method which the British developed for use with the early tanks crossing trench lines in World War I. If time permits, plant equipment, or dozer blades mounted on tanks can push the spoil back into the ditch. Both NATO and the Warsaw Pact have dozer blade attachments for tanks and they are also very useful in enhancing AFV fire positions. The third method is using a bridgelayer tank, and some of these will accompany the leading engineers in a Soviet advance, along with mine plough and dozer tanks. There are three basic types. There is the straight forward bridge for short gaps – the Soviet MTU-1 with a span of 12m and mounted on a T-54 chassis. The cantilever bridge, which is carried with the two end sections folded on top of the middle, is represented by the Soviet MTU-20, which is on a T-55 chassis and has a 20m span. Finally, there is the scissors bridge for wider gaps, and this is the most popular with both alliances. The US M60 Armored Vehicle

Above left: Soviet TMM 60 ton scissors bridge. A bridge set is four spans and can cover a 40m gap.
Below left: Soviet GSP ferry with a T-55 tank. Only four minutes are needed to put it into operation.
Above: Canadian Leopard bridgelayer.
Below: US Engineers construct a Ribbon Bridge.

Launched Bridge (AVLB) has a span of just over 18m, while the British Chieftain AVLB can cover 23m. The Warsaw Pact armies rely on the East German BLG-60 (T-55 chassis, 21.6m span) and the Czech MT-55 (T-55 chassis, 18m span). In all cases the bridge is laid hydraulically and takes 2–5 minutes to place in position. The tank will then retire behind cover and wait until it can retrieve the bridge again.

Other types of artificial obstacle include chopping down trees onto forest rides, the cratering of roads and blowing down houses in urban areas. If time permits, natural obstacles can be enhanced. Slopes can be made steeper so that AFVs cannot climb up them, and the banks of rivers and canals made steeper so that amphibious vehicles cannot enter or exit. In places it is possible to cause flooding. However, unless some of these measures can, where acceptable to the local population, be carried out in peacetime, it is most unlikely that NATO engineers will have sufficient time to carry out more than local route denial. What, however, is important is that minefields, demolitions and other obstacles are properly recorded. Unless friendly troops know of their location, they will suffer both mobility problems and casualties,

Left: East German built BLG-60 scissors bridge on T-55 chassis on a GSP ferry.
Top: Constructing a GSP ferry.
Above: British Chieftain bridgelayer.

173

apart from the problems of clearing minefields after the war is over.

The Central Region is crisscrossed by numerous rivers, streams and canals. These provide ideal natural obstacles, and are of particular concern to the Soviets. Their first thought would be to try and seize bridges still intact over the river, before they reach it. This would be a typical objective for a heliborne or even, if the obstacle was a formidable one, the air assault brigade, airborne troops or the OMG. If they were unable to do this or it was not considered feasible, the next option would be to try a 'bounce crossing' off the line of march, and finally a deliberate crossing. In all this, the most important role is that of the engineers. The first task is reconnaissance. Although they will have detailed technical information about the river and likely crossing places, the engineers will still need to confirm the state of the river, new obstacles and defenses, including mines. Using BRDMs, they will carry out a detailed technical reconnaissance, not just in the area where the crossing is to be made, but over a long stretch of the river in order not to indicate the likely crossing places to the enemy. A Division will usually require four crossing points.

In terms of actually crossing the river, the first stage is to secure a lodgement on the far bank. This will usually be done by motor rifle elements swimming their vehicles across under the cover of both direct and indirect fire and smoke. It may be, however, that the entry and/or exit banks are unsuitable for this, in which case they will be transported across on special amphibious load carrying vehicles – the PTS-M and the older and smaller K-61. Once the bridgehead is established ferries, usually the GSP, will bring across tanks to give added support to the bridgehead and, in conjunction with additional motor rifle elements and self-propelled artillery, to continue the advance. Finally, floating bridges will be put in.

The main floating bridge employed by the Soviets is the PMP, which was first seen in operational use by the West during the Egyptian crossing of the Suez Canal in 1973. It is made up of a number of pontoons, which are each transported folded on a KrAZ-255B truck. They are offloaded into the river, unfolded and then married up together, with the assistance of power boats. A complete bridge set consists of 32 river and four shore pontoons, but is normally used in a halfset and manned by a pontoon company. A halfset can be laid in some thirty minutes and will span 110m, giving a weight capacity of 60 tonnes. The older TMM bridge is also still in service, and airborne forces use the PVD-20, which is air droppable and will take loads up to 8 tonnes. NATO floating bridges have an advantage over their Pact rivals in that the vehicles which transport the pontoon sections are themselves amphibious and make up the floating supports for the bridge, which can be assembled and dismantled in a faster time. The first of these to appear was the German M2 floating bridge, which was bought by the British, but the US has recently introduced the aluminum Ribbon Bridge, which is even quicker to assemble, and has been adopted by the Germans.

Because of the vulnerability of bridges to air attack, the normal practise on both sides is to assemble them at last light and dismantle them again before first light. Thus a crossing might well take place over two or even more nights. Vehicles waiting to cross will remain in hides until called forward, and this needs an efficient control system. In the Soviet Army this is done by the engineers themselves, but NATO armies prefer to use other units for this task, which is often given to reconnaissance units. Another aspect which has to be carefully watched is the state of the approaches to the bridge on either side, and trackway will often be used to prevent the ground from becoming too churned up, resulting in bogged vehicles. By the same token, the means to recover vehicles which have broken down close to the bridge need to be readily available. A final point is that, although the

Previous page: British multi-role amphibious Combat Engineer Tractor.
Left: A Chinook delivers plant equipment to British Royal Engineers.
Below: US M577 armored command vehicle crossing a Dutch pontoon bridge.
Bottom: Soviet 110 ton ferry constructed from PMP equipment.

ability of Soviet tanks to deep ford using schnorkelling kit has been much publicized in the past, it is very dangerous and there have been numerous accidents. Hence the Soviets are very unlikely to employ this crossing method unless nothing else is available. Even then, it will only be attempted after a very careful inspection of both the banks and river bottom by frogmen.

Further back from the battle area there will be a constant need to maintain crossings across obstacles, especially if they have been subjected to air attack. In the Warsaw Pact rear areas these are the responsibility of the Military Road Troops and Construction Troops, two separate military branches from the combat engineers. They have available a wide range of barge and girder bridges and even a combined road and railway bridge. In NATO armies there is not this differentiation in services, and it is still an engineer responsibility.

Up until recently, NATO engineers have suffered from a shortage of modern equipment and have found it ever more difficult to carry out their tasks effectively. One of the main problems is that they have had to be reliant on ordinary APCs for much of their work, and these have proved very unsatisfactory. As a result a number of light armored vehicles have been especially designed for the combat engineer, and including dozer, winch and crane devices. Typical of this new type of vehicle is the British Combat Engineer Tractor (CET) and the US M9 armored dozer, which is just entering service with the US Army. The Germans, too, are developing a specialist engineer vehicle based on the Leopard 2 chassis. The Soviets also have the IMR Combat Engineer Vehicle (CEV), which is on a T-55 chassis.

Another valuable engineer role is that of assisting the forward troops in constructing field defenses, especially in the construction of weapons positions and dugouts. Cratering kits, like the US M180, which can create a hole 2m deep by 9m across in 30 minutes, enable effective defenses to be prepared very much more quickly than hitherto, and the introduction of prefabricated devices to enhance protection is going some way to counter the ever increasing weight of fire which can be brought down on field defenses. The engineers of both sides also advise on camouflage, and the Soviets have special camouflage companies at army level who can also construct dummy trenches and vehicles. Other tasks include water supply and purification and the construction of Petrol, Oil and Lubricants (POL) pipelines and storage facilities.

The engineers on both sides have much to contribute to the battle, which for them will be one of mobility versus countermobility. The extent to which NATO and the Warsaw Pact are able to fight the high speed battle to which they both aspire will depend very greatly on the success and failure of the combat engineers.

10. LOGISTICS

Air resupply – C-130 Hercules delivers palletized supplies
using the Low Altitude Parachute Extraction System
(LAPES).

Admiral Ernest J King, the US Naval Chief of Naval Operations during World War II, who masterminded the war at sea against Japan, once remarked, 'I don't know what the hell this "logistics" is that Marshall (Chairman US Joint Chiefs of Staff) is always talking about, but I want some of it'. In a nutshell, it is the supplying and maintaining of forces in the field. Although it is widely considered as the 'unglamorous' side of war, without an efficient logistics system an army will 'wither on the vine', as Admiral King recognized.

Logistics embraces a wide range of subjects from vehicle repair, the supply of clothing and the provision of radio batteries to the treatment of wounded and prisoners of war, mail and the supply of reinforcements. They can, however, be broken down into two broad categories – equipment and personnel.

In terms of supplies, the three essential items that any army needs to continue fighting are ammunition, POL and food. Probable ammunition expenditure, especially by artillery, is likely to be very high in World War III. Since the average self-propelled gun seldom has a carrying capacity of more than fifty rounds and is likely to move frequently, much of an artillery unit's immediate reserves of ammunition has to be kept on wheels. One problem with this is the vulnerability of soft skinned vehicles in the battle area, and the US Army is solving this by means of the field artillery ammunition support vehicle (FAASV). This is an armored vehicle which can carry 93 rounds of 155mm or 48 rounds of 203mm. Using an automatic

stacker and hydraulic conveyor, the rounds can be passed to the gun without the crews of either vehicle having to get out and expose themselves to enemy fire. Nevertheless, there is never sufficient transport to keep all ammunition on wheels, and much has to be dumped. The tendency is increasingly to use hardened underground sites which have been constructed in peacetime. In order to decide how much ammunition is required, both sides calculate average daily expenditure rates and stock accordingly. At present NATO maintains stocks for some thirty days in theater, while the Warsaw Pact is reputed to base its holdings on forty days.

If the war is to be as mobile as both sides envisage, consumption of POL is going to be very high. Both sides will construct pipelines as far forward as possible, but fuel will have to be transported by truck to the forward troops. In the past, fuel was normally put in jerricans. The major advantage of these was the ability for POL to be manhandled to forward positions. However, replenishment with them takes time. Instead, almost all armies now use bowsers, which can refuel as many as four vehicles simultaneously, and what is called 'running' replenishment is carried out. The POL vehicles travel to a prearranged rendezvous, and the unit to be replenished passes through, taking on fuel and ammunition as it does so. Because of the air threat, replenishment of forward units is almost invariably done by night.

Most armies believe in centralized cooking, although the British are a notable exception. Each

Left: Soviet ZIL-131 6 × 6 truck.
Above: US 8 × 8 M985 cargo truck.

company has its field kitchen and food is cooked here and then distributed to the troops when the fighting allows. In the British Army, however, combat and combat support units rely on vehicle cooking, with each crew being issued its rations and doing its cooking on electrical cookers provided with the AFV. This is a much simpler system, and does guarantee that soldiers will get at least one hot meal per day, an important consideration in terms of morale. The US Army, is, however, in the process of replacing its familiar C rations with the 'meal ready to eat', which requires much less cooking, and may well lead to more vehicle catering in the forward zone. A point worth mentioning is that no NATO army has the same rations, and that the soldier tends to be very conservative in his food tastes. Using each other's rations would therefore be acceptable only for very short periods.

With high combat vehicle attrition rates, recovery and repair is vital. The armies of both sides have mechanics at company level in their mechanized units. Their main tasks are vehicle recovery and minor repairs which are beyond the limitations of the crews. Both the Germans in North Africa and the Russians on the Eastern Front during World War II recognized the importance of recovering vehicle casualties from the battlefield in order to maintain strength in armor. Often it was found that relatively simple repairs were all that was needed to make AFVs

fit again, but also, as the Soviets recognize, where spare parts are difficult to obtain, vehicle casualties can often be cannabilized in order to repair other vehicles. All NATO and Warsaw Pact armies use the armored recovery vehicle (ARV), which is normally a tank chassis with a winch and sometimes a crane for lifting major assemblies. Casualties, if they cannot be repaired by the unit, will normally be backloaded for second line repair. For the side which is advancing, this will merely mean taking them to a central point where they would wait for second line repair units to arrive. In withdrawal, however, the problem is more difficult, and repair units will have to identify those vehicles which can be easily repaired and abandon the remainder, since the number of recovery vehicles will be limited. One area, however, in which first line repairs are becoming very much more simple is electronic and communication equipment. Often it is merely a question of replacing modules.

Logistic vehicles operating in the forward area need to be highly mobile, especially as they might well have to travel across country. Although all military trucks have drive to all wheels, which enables them to move off roads, they can only travel slowly cross-country. The answer to this is the High Mobility Load Carrier (HMLC), designed specifically for movement off the road. The British were the first to enter this field when they introduced the Stalwart in the mid Sixties. The Soviets have the ZIL-135, which was originally designed for transporting the Shaddock and Frog-7 missiles. The best of this type of vehicle in

the Warsaw Pact is, however, the Czech 8 tonne 8 X 8 Tatra 813. The West Germans now have the Transportpanzer Fuchs, a multirole armored vehicle, which uses many of the Luchs reconnaissance vehicle components. The US Army has developed the Hummer, which will replace most of its jeeps and Gama Goat trucks, and is introducing an entirely new truck fleet.

Turning to personnel, casualty treatment and evacuation is perhaps the most important aspect. Even if World War III remains conventional, casualties are likely to be very high on both sides. They will not occur just from gunshot wounds, mines, shrapnel, burns and blast, but also from chemical attack. Furthermore, shell shock or battle fatigue casualties are likely to be high in view of the concentration of fire to which front line troops will be subjected. Thus the medical services of both sides will be very stretched, and should the fighting turn nuclear, the situation will be even worse. At the very lowest level, as the British learnt in the Falklands, much can be done if every man is well trained in First Aid. Normally, there is at company level a medic with an armored ambulance, and the first task is to recover the casualty and give him immediate First Aid. He is then taken back to battalion, where there is a medical officer. Every man usually carries a field dressing and a morphine syrette, and if he has been given the latter, this must be noted – it is normally written on his forehead. The medical officer will diagnose his injuries and redress his wounds. The next stage is then to get him back to a collecting

Top: Soviet BMP company refueling. Bowsers will be used in forward areas.
Above: T-62 climbs aboard a MAZ-537 tank transporter.
Above right: A Soviet field hospital.
Right: In order to save track wear, tanks will, where possible, use tank transporters or railroad for long moves in rear areas. These are M60A1s.

station in the rear. This will be done by armored ambulance or ideally, if available, helicopter. At the collecting station, casualties will be sorted into categories and those requiring surgery are taken to what, in US Army terms, is called a Mobile Army Surgical Hospital (MASH), which is situated in the divisional rear area. From then on, the patient is taken back by stages to a base hospital. This is the outline system used by NATO armies, and the Soviet system is roughly similar, although it is questionable whether the Warsaw Pact soldier will receive the same standard of treatment and attention.

Prisoner of War (PW) handling is also likely to be a problem in a fast moving battle. On initial capture, PWs are searched and interrogated. The latter can result in valuable intelligence, since the PW is likely to be in a state of shock and may well volunteer information without realizing that he has done so. This is even though the Geneva Convention allows a man only to give his name, rank, number and religion. It is then important to pass PWs back as quickly as possible. For a start, combat troops can be ill afforded to look after PWs. Also, the closer to the front line, the more the opportunities for the PW to escape. Officer PWs and others likely to have valuable information will be brought up in front of specialist battle interrogation teams. It should be noted, however, that any information on future plans and operations which a PW captured on the battlefield might have will probably be out of date within 24 hours.

Refugees may severely restrict the movement of troops unless they are properly controlled. During the campaign in France and the Low Countries in May 1940, the sheer mass of people fleeing from the Germans often forced military units off the roads. In the Central Region, the civil population will be encouraged as much as possible to stay put in their houses, but it is unlikely that this will be more than partially heeded, especially by those living near the border with the East. Civil police are mainly responsible for refugee control, but in the forward areas this will often have to be done by military police. Refugees will be allocated routes selected to interfere as little as possible with military movement, and it is then a question of trying to keep them to these routes and to ensure that they keep moving. It is likely to be no easy task, especially when panic can spread like wild fire.

As for those routes required specifically for military purposes, these are designated, in NATO parlance, Main Supply Routes (MSR). As their name suggests, these will be the main logistic arteries for the forward troops, and it is important that they are kept open the whole time. One of the enemy's tasks will be to disrupt them, and hence they will need to be guarded by mobile patrols and static guards at vulnerable points such as bridges. Engineer

support will have to be readily available in case they are blocked by damage, and diversions put into effect while they are being repaired. In corps rear areas and further behind, their protection will be a prime task for rear area security forces. As with movement in the forward areas, resupply convoys will only travel the MSRs by night, because of the air threat.

Both NATO and the Warsaw Pact have large static logistic installations well to the rear, where are held what is known in NATO as the War Maintenance Reserve (WMR). These contain everything required to fight the war and, while probably not more than seven days worth is held with corps or Warsaw Pact armies, the balance is held in these depots. The NATO depots, which each member nation has, are either in national territory or, in the case of overseas countries, as the USA, UK and Canada are in the Central Region, within theater. The Warsaw Pact has a very large depot at Grossborn in Poland, with subsidiaries in the GDR, Czechoslovakia and Hungary. When these stores are outloaded they will be moved by rail, water or road forward to the corps area and then broken down into divisional slices in corps dumps. The Warsaw Pact is especially reliant on railroads, which are not as dense as those in Western Europe and hence make obvious targets for air attack. They will run right up to the armies, and each of the latter will have a railhead, where the supplies are then crossloaded onto trucks. One significant point is that, although Eastern European railroads are a wider gauge than in the West, the Soviets keep stocks of conversion kits close to the borders. In this way they can, once the advance has penetrated deep enough take advantage of the FRG railroad system.

In NATO eyes at least, the ability to mobilize and reinforce quickly is going to be vital. In the Central Region this is less of a problem for the Germans, Dutch and Belgians since the distances involved are comparatively short. For the British, and more especially Canada and the US, the problem is much more severe, and this is where the Soviets have an initial advantage. Indeed, they are fully aware of NATO's dependence on reinforcements from overseas, and it is another reason why they strive for a quick victory. The more forces NATO is able to deploy, the harder it will be for them.

The initial NATO priority for reinforcements will be those earmarked to bring front line divisions up to strength. These can either be individual or unit reinforcements. The former are for units and formations already in place and are normally additional staff officers or specialists. As for the latter, USAREUR's prime concern will be the bringing across from CONUS of the two brigades each for

Top: Intertheater moves of armor will normally be done by tank landing ship. A T-72 disembarks.
Right: Strategic airlift is also used. Here a SCUD missile launcher leaves an Antonov An-22 Cub transport.

Left: US Army air traffic control center for coordinating aircraft in the corps area.
Below left: Soviet Mi-10 Harke heavy lift helicopter with a 15 ton payload.
Below: Helicopter handler supervises the recovery of a Bell OH-58 scout helicopter by a CH-47 Chinook.

3rd and 4th Mechanized Infantry Divisions. The Germans will be mobilizing their Territorial Command, while the British bring across the reinforcing infantry battalions for their three armored divisions and deploy 2nd Infantry Division from UK. The Dutch and Belgians will be bringing the elements of their corps which are stationed on national territory up to strength and moving them into the corps areas. In terms of the calling up of reserves, the conscript armies have an advantage over those which are volunteer in that they have a larger pool of trained manpower to call upon. Thus the Dutch, for example, retain their conscripts for two years on the reserve after they have completed their active duty, and have them already organized into units, which carry out a period of training each year. The US Army has recently evolved the concept of the Total Army. This is aimed at binding the National Guard and Army Reserve more closely to the Regular Army, with much more integration than hitherto. In general, National Guard units are organized into combat divisions and brigades, while the Army Reserve provides individual reinforcements and units to strengthen regular formations. Most of the latter are in the combat support, combat service support and general support roles, although there are some combat units. The British Regular Army reserves are earmarked as individual reinforcements, while the Territorial Army provides formed units and brigades and indeed makes up the greater part of 2nd Infantry Division. The Canadians will look to the Militia.

Reinforcements from CONUS will come initially by air, flying in MAC's C-5 Galaxies, C-130 Hercules and C-141 Starlifters. Civil airliners will also be commandeered for use as well. For those regular units which are permanently earmarked for the Central Region, which include III (US) Corps, made up of 1st Cavalry Division, 2nd Armored Division, 1st, 4th and 5th Mechanized Infantry Divisions, 6th Cavalry (Air Combat) Brigade and 3rd Armored Cavalry Regiment, their vehicles and equipment are already in theater. Under a new system, Prepositioned Material Configured to Unit Sets (POMCUS), which operates on the same principle as the US Marine Corps prepositioned ships in the Indian Ocean, units arriving in the Central Region from CONUS draw up complete sets of vehicles and equipment, thus very significantly reducing the time needed to prepare them. CONUS formations have the opportunity to confirm POMCUS during the annual *Reforger* maneuvers which involve airlifting units from CONUS to Europe. Although the airlift is vital for speedy reinforcement, the majority of National Guard and Army Reserve units will come by sea, along with their equipment, and will begin embarking about thirty days after mobilization has been called. Indeed, 90%

Above: Railroads will be important for bringing in reinforcements.
Above right: US C-5 Galaxy which will play a crucial part in flying reinforcements from CONUS to Europe.

of the total lift across the Atlantic will be by sea.

Most of the shipping will be taken up from trade. Reinforcements from the UK across the English Channel will also go by air and sea, with again ships, especially Cross Channel ferries, being taken up from trade as will civil aircraft. The British Army, however, having a shorter distance to travel, does not have a system like POMCUS.

Apart from reinforcements to strengthen the order of battle, there is also the need to cater for vehicle and personnel replacements for those who have become casualties. In the Warsaw Pact, the echelon system, whereby divisions continue in action until they have suffered 50% casualties or more, means that replacements take the form of formations rather than individual replacements. Thus, once the 1st echelon divisions have become exhausted, the 2nd echelon will take over, while the remains of the 1st will be refitted and requipped over a period of time. NATO, having fewer divisions available, will try and keep them topped up with replacements. Each corps will have reinforcement units, to which many of the individual reinforcements will initially report. Those who have been sick or wounded, but are now recovered will also be fed back into the battle through this means. Other units will hold stocks of guns and AFVs and, wherever possible, complete crews will take vehicles forward and reinforce depleted units.

This has been very much a broad look at logistics as they affect the land battle, alighting on some of the more important aspects. There are a number of other areas, including pay, postal services and even canteens, which have not been covered, but each in its own way helps towards the overall aim of enhancing the combat power of the forward troops. For a logistics system to function effectively, it must be able to anticipate the needs of those whom it is supporting so that the right supplies arrive at the right place at the right time. It must be economic so that supplies and especially transport, of which there will never be enough, are not needlessly squandered. The system must be flexible in order to cope with the unexpected, which will always occur in war. Logistic plans and systems must also be kept as simple as possible and, above all, good cooperation among staffs, combat and service support troops is required. World War III is likely to test the systems of both sides to the limit and beyond, but the side which adheres most closely to these principles is the one which is most likely to win.

11. THE OUTCOME?

This book has tried to give an idea of the equipment, strategy and tactics of the armies of the Warsaw Pact and NATO, and how they might fight World War III in the Central Region. Some of the strengths and weaknesses have been highlighted, but as to what the outcome of World War III in Europe would be is hard to judge.

For a start, both sides hope to achieve their aims through peaceful means, and the Soviet Union will only go to war if she feels militarily threatened and cannot attain her goals by any other way. In any event, she will only go to war if she is certain that she can win it, and win it quickly. Thus, so long as the NATO deterrent remains strong, war between the two alliances is unlikely to occur in the foreseeable future. It would only come if one side or the other makes a serious miscalculation. If this did happen, then the first question would be whether it could be fought without recourse to tactical nuclear weapons.

NATO's current policy is to use nuclear weapons if the conventional ground forces cannot hold the Warsaw Pact attacks. In this case, NATO planners are well aware of the attendant dangers of precipitating a global nuclear exchange, and hence the efforts being made to strengthen conventional NATO defenses. Conversely, the Soviets would also prefer to fight a conventional war, but it must be won quickly. If this was not happening and/or they had failed to knock out NATO's tactical nuclear missile launchers, the temptation to initiate a nuclear strike might be very strong, but the decision as to whether or not to do this will be very much influenced by their perceptions of the NATO will to escalate the conflict in retaliation.

Even if the war does remain conventional, it is generally accepted that the Soviet Union would use chemical warfare from the outset, albeit nonpersistent. The US is taking steps to modernize her chemical weapon stocks, and hence it is probable that she will retaliate, after having obtained agreement from her fellow NATO members. Again, she is likely to employ only nonpersistent agents as otherwise NATO operations, especially counterattack and deep counterthrust, might be impeded. Besides the possible use of nuclear and almost certain use of chemical weapons, however, modern technology is producing conventional weapons which have the potential to be just as lethal.

In particular, the PGM is about to give a radically new complexion to the land battle. Furthermore, there are even more devastating weapons which will appear very shortly. Fuel Air Explosive (FAE) devices which, on detonation, produce very high overpressures, can cause physical destruction equivalent to that of a tactical nuclear weapon. The US Army is introducing this shortly in the form of a remotely delivered minefield clearing device, SLUFAE (Surface Launched Fuel Air Explosive Mine Neutralization System). The laser, too, is likely to become more of a battlefield weapon than just a target acquisition means. At the end of 1983, it was reported that the US was developing a system called C-Claw, which uses lasers to cripple human and mechanical optics. The Soviets also are reputed to have a similar system called Tin Man, a naval weapon designed to blind submarine hunting helicopters. There is, too, the neutron bomb, which kills more by radiation than blast, and either side might be tempted to use this, especially if it could convince itself that it was not a nuclear weapon. These new types of weapon system therefore make it difficult to envisage what the land battlefield might be like beyond the very near future.

Nevertheless, the new weapons systems coming into service at present, combined with the striving by both sides to develop C^3I systems which will produce 'real time' intelligence, point to the fact that the speed and tempo of the land battle will be increasingly faster. NATO is pinning its hopes on maintaining a lead over its rival in high technology, and to use this as a conventional force multiplier. If its intelligence is more timely than that of its enemy, it will have a significant advantage, and this, together with the new weapons systems, might well offset its current numerical inferiority.

It must not be forgotten, however, that, even in this age of ever more sophisticated technology, that there is still, and always will be, a large element of chance in war, and that ultimately it is the human being who has to make the decisions. It will still be the ability of the soldier to think and act more quickly than his opponent which will win land battles of the future.

INDEX

The publisher would like to thank Adrian Hodgkins who designed this book, Ron Watson for preparing the index, The Royal Ordnance Factory and the individuals and agencies listed below for providing the photographs:

AP Worldwide pp 14 (top), 15, 16, 17, 31 (top)
Bison Picture Library pp 31, 32, 34, 35, 73, 91 (top), 136 (bottom)
British Aerospace p 123 (both)
Canadair p 127
Canadian Defence Forces pp 26-27, 35, 37 (bottom), 43, 86-87, 90 (top), 95 (bottom), 97 (bottom), 105 (top), 107 (top), 111 (bottom), 133, 137 (bottom), 146 (bottom), 171 (top), 178-179
Central Press p 12 (top)
FMC Corporation pp 70 (bottom), 103 (bottom)
General Dynamics pp 142-143, 149 (bottom)
Harco Corp pp 106 (top)
Hughes Aircraft Co pp 97 (top), 124
Robert Hunt Library pp 9, 10, 11, 73 (bottom)
Imperial War Museum pp 8 (top), 12 (bottom)
MARS pp 36, 63, 66-67, 78 (top right), 85, 88 (bottom), 93 (below right), 96, 99 (both), 105 (bottom), 111 (top), 161
Martin Marietta pp 120
Charles Messenger p 176
MOD pp 18, 46-47, 48, 49 (top), 72, 82, 83 (bottom), 92 (bottom), 108-109, 113, 136 (top), 152 (top), 157, 160, 164, 165, 166, 167 (top), 168 (top), 173 (top), 174-175
Novosti pp 8 (bottom), 14 (top), 21 (bottom), 28, 29, 68, 69 (bottom), 138 (both), 139, 144, 156, 173 (bottom), 177 (bottom), 185 (bottom), 186 (bottom)
Rockwell International p 149 (top)
Shorts p 121 (top right)
TASS p 185 (top)
US Army pp 6-7, 13, 19, 22, 24, 32, 33 (bottom), 38 (top two), 39 (top), 40, 41, 42 (top), 45, 50-51, 52, 54, 55, 56, 57, 58-59, 61, 62 (both), 63, 65, 69 (top), 70 (top), 71, 76 (bottom), 77, 78-79 (bottom and top left), 83 (top), 88 (top), 89 (all three), 90 (bottom right), 91 (bottom), 92 (top), 93 (below left), 98, 101, 102 (both), 107 (bottom), 116 (top two), 117 (both), 119 (all three), 121 (top left and below), 122, 123 (top), 128-129, 130-131 (all three), 132 (all three), 134, 135 (both), 137 (top), 141 (both), 153; 158-159, 162-163, 167 (bottom), 168 (bottom), 169, 170 (both), 171 (bottom), 172 (top), 177 (top), 180, 181, 182 (both), 183 (both), 186, 187, 188, 189 (top)
US Defense Department pp 23 (top), 53, 76 (top left), 81 (both), 93 (top), 95 (top two), 100 (both), 103 (top), 104 (both), 106 (bottom), 114, 115, 124, 126, 144, 146 (top), 147 (top right and bottom), 150-151, 152 (bottom), 153, 154, 155
US Air Force p 49 (bottom)
US Marine Corps p 94 (bottom)
US Navy 116 (bottom)
Vought Corp p 113